Bless

Jim Mo

A Journey of Reflections

Lessons Along The Way

Jim Moeller

Serenity

Www.SerenityMusic.Com

Printed in the United States of America

Library of Congress Control Number

ISBN 1-881614-05-0

Cover Photo: "Backroad Through Owens Valley" by Galen Rowell/ Mountain Light. www.mountainlight.com

Graphic Design: Steve Johnson and Ken Moeller
Graphic Concept: Jim Moeller

Published by Serenity: www.SerenityMusic.com

For more information on this book and on Serenity's music albums: www.SerenityMusic.com

To Contact Jim Moeller: jmoeller@serenitymusic.com

This book is dedicated to:

Chad and Jason Moeller, my sons,

Linda Moeller, their mother, and

Mom and Dad.

They, more than anyone,
felt the pain of my past.

Thank You

Few projects would ever make it beyond mental concept if it were not for the help of others. This book is no different.

Starting with the first word written, Judy Link and Carolyn Weyant had the willingness to read, reread, correct, suggest, and in general, put up with me. I would imagine both had to wonder how I ever passed an English grammar class.

As I continued to write, I knew that I needed to expand upon the many thoughts that I was putting to paper. In search of help I:

-Put the words "creative writing" into Google to find a possible class in my area. Magically (or should I say, God working anonymously), at the top of the list was a class at the University of California, Riverside, less than 20 miles away and starting five days later.

-Asked my youngest son, an English teacher, to set aside my parenthood to become an objective reader and to make suggestions about my writing.

If any of my words have reason to motivate you to greater thinking, much of the thanks must go to Mike Foley, the professor at University of California, Riverside, and Jason Moeller, my son. Both showed me ways to take "words" and give them "life."

To several others. They listened to what I was proposing and helped make it a financial reality. Without their help, the writing for this book would have remained in journals on my shelf.

Author's Note

As you read the following pages, you will see where I make reference to some my mentors. In all honesty, each moment lived, each person met, each book read, and each situation experienced is potentially a learning moment, a moment of mentoring. However, there are three people that I wish to acknowledge because of their continual influence in my life.

Dr. Robert Merkle. We first met when I attended one of his classes in the early 1980's at **The Crystal Cathedral**, the longtime church of Dr. Robert Schuller in Garden Grove, California. At that time Dr. Merkle was the Director of Counseling for the entire church. In the years that followed not only did I attend at least a hundred of his classes and seminars, he became my advisor as I worked toward my Ph.D. in Counseling Psychology.

Mike Slaughter—Pastor of the Ginghamsburg United Methodist Church in Ginghamsburg, Ohio. At the recommendation of a friend, I drove the 60 miles to attend one of his Sunday church services. So moved was I that I continued to make the same drive each Sunday until my relocation to California. When I left, I sent Mike a note telling him that "I would have never thought that I would ever tell someone how much I was going to miss my church." I not only missed my church, but Mike's wisdom as well. He reintroduced me to a God I had never before experienced.

Dan Carroll—Pastor of the Water of Life Church in Fontana, California. Again, at the recommendation of a friend, I attended one of his services. I was truly blessed to find another church beyond description. Among the many lessons Dan is continuing to teach me is, "It's not about religion, it's about a relationship with God."

I need to add this disclaimer. These three have stirred me to think more deeply about many spiritual issues but, under no circumstance should one assume that they agree with what I have written.

Foreword

Jim Moeller's book, ***A Journey of Reflections***, came into my life like so many of my most cherished spiritual events—unsought and totally timely. My husband, Michael, was helping Jim with some editing and knew I would enjoy reading the book. He was absolutely right.

I'm probably not much different than most people in that my concept of giving and volunteering myself is something linked to pressure and the clock—something to do when I've reduced a sufficient amount of stress and time-consuming irritants. But that free time never seems to come, further defining the process of giving as "not now." Sound familiar? This, of course, adds to the growing feelings of guilt and inadequacy, making us feel worse, not better.

So what can we do? Jim's book is a good start.

Unlike my experience with most spiritual books and belief systems, I read this book and found myself agreeing with every idea, every suggestion. I remember marveling as I suddenly realized that it wouldn't matter which church you attended or which spiritual path you identified with. Jim's book is universally applicable to all. It's a marvelous spiritual journey, free of dogma, "shoulds," and "shame on yous."

Jim has a way of showing us that our lives really aren't so complex, that service is something which can happen naturally—a simple, automatic reaction to simplifying our priorities. How did this affect me? Inspired by Jim's daily routine, I found myself running again for the first time in years. And later, I checked in at the local blood mobile and donated blood, despite the fact that I had convinced myself I was too old for it, that the simple act of giving was just too much to ask.

As I reflect back on these changes, I realize that simply by opening myself, I had begun considering Jim's spiritual message as a viable option in my life. And as a result, my life has flowed differently, with a new sense of possibility.

After reading ***A Journey of Reflections***, I found myself reflecting on how susceptible we are to everyday messages, especially those that bombard us from all directions through the media, the challenges of friends and family, and the stress of work. That's why this book is so important. It is nothing less than a reminder of why we're really here. Picking up this book and reading it is a profound and loving act that can change your life and alter your path.

Consider the possibilities in these pages. Take them into your life and act according to your heart. That's the only thing required here. I hope that, like me, you'll rediscover a new sense of purpose.

May it bring you a lifetime of joy.

Martha Foley
Big Bear City, CA
May, 2006

Prologue

Over 25 years ago I sat face to face with Wendy, an alcoholism counselor at a treatment center in Wickenburg, Arizona, called The Meadows. She looked me in the eye as she firmly yelled, "Jim, you're going to have to make a choice. You're going to have to decide if you want to live or die!"

She was not a counselor who took her job lightly. By the end of my five week stay, she had called me every "foul language" four-letter word invented. Not once, but nearly every day.

By the end of my stay, she ordered me out of street clothes and back into pajamas several times as she tried to emphasize how sick I was.

Before I finished my five weeks at the center, she had thrown me out of my chair, forcing me to sit silently on the floor to help break down my powerful ego. On occasion, this same chair would fly over my head crashing into a wall as she tried to emphasize a point.

Before I left The Meadows, Wendy also introduced me to the art of journaling, demanding that I dig more deeply to uncover my hidden self. I didn't know it then, but this book began its gestation on the day she ordered me to carry a pencil and pad everywhere I went.

Battling alcoholism is only one part of my life that has swayed in the winds of both good and bad. I was blessed to have been introduced to a 12-Step program that has remained my closest ally in this "one day at a time battle."

I am very much aware of what it means to acknowledge that I am in a 12-Step program. Anonymity is a cornerstone of these types of programs, but long ago I learned that I need not try to conceal my heavy drinking since everyone already knew it.

What is important for all readers to understand is that the 12-Step program that I will refer to throughout my book has kept me, and millions of others, alive. However, if the day ever comes that I again choose to drink, it will not be the fault of the 12-Step program. It will be my decision to return to my old ways of ego and alcohol, and the false gods associated with that decision. For what it is worth, since March 12, 1980, each day I've been faced with that choice, and each day my decision has been to choose "sobriety and God over alcohol and ego."

Although 12-Step programs are normally associated with alcoholism and drug abuse, the program, with minor word changes, is used by hundreds of organizations around the world. Over time I have become convinced that the 12-Steps used in all of the 12-Step programs could be a cornerstone in each of our daily lives. Someone along the way rewrote the steps in only six words:

-Trust God,

-Clean house,

-Help others.

Although a daily student of a 12-Step program, many inputs, both "good and bad," represent who I 've become.

Not only was I fortunate to have caring parents, I had two sets of caring grandparents living within a few miles of my home.

Because one set of grandparents owned a farm, in early childhood a large amount of time living there, learning the value of work. In fact, one of my earliest farm memories was driving the tractor and running down a corner-post along with the 10-foot gate attached to it. On that same day I learned how to round up 25 milk cows.

Many parts of me that I would consider "good" were due to the strength of a loving family in my early life.

But, in spite of strong family values, by the time I reached high school age, I had already experienced numerous blackouts and had been arrested for buying beer at a tavern. Couple that with "borrowing" a person's car, without permission, at age 15 (the court called it stealing) and you can see where I was headed.

By the end of high school, my alcohol use had grown causing several auto accidents. In addition, it cost me numerous athletic scholarships to some of the most prestigious schools in the Midwest.

What was truly a miracle is that I graduated from The Ohio State University with a degree in Aeronautical Engineering. Unfortunately, more Columbus bartenders than professors knew me by my first name.

The military came next. After more than a thousand hours of flying high performance jets, many on and off aircraft carriers, coupled with another degree, a Masters' in engineering, I had a realistic dream of becoming an astronaut.

The dream ended when I subconsciously chose alcohol over commitment.

After giving up the dream of outer space, I entered the civilian workforce, and before long, I was on a corporate fast track until alcohol-laced decisions led to my dismissal.

If the business world did not want me, then I would choose a path of self-employment. If one is an alcoholic, there is no faster way to spiral downward than to buy the dream business of every alcoholic, a liquor store.

Soon after, my abusive words and actions caused the end of my marriage—and a day-to-day relationship with my sons.

The proverbial "bottom" finally arrived while living in a "low-rent" room furnished with a mattress on the floor and a small black and white TV.

Sobriety can lead to many changes, the biggest coming when one reverses a journey that was pointed in the wrong direction for decades. Healing starts to blossom as one retraces the steps, no matter how painful. There are no shortcuts. It is the undoing of all the destruction done both to others, as well as to "self." I call it the journey of amends.

For me it has been this lengthy relationship in a 12-Step program coupled with another Masters' Degree, this time in Counseling Psychology. With these tools I was able to work with an untold number of families as I continued to dismantle my "ego" self.

Retracing these steps of the past does not prevent new challenges, many requiring even tougher decisions than before. Invariably, more bad decisions can, and are made. That is part of being human in a fast-paced world. The difference now is that I, most times, try to correct my mistakes immediately.

Additional choices, many decided deep within the heart and hard for others to understand, had a major impact on the lives of others, like anonymously donating a kidney to someone I had never met.

In 1985 I founded a music label with a business plan of creating music for relaxation. This has brought thousands of hurting people into my life. In each of their pain, I see me. In each of their pain, I see an opportunity for God to use me to help another.

The bottom line is this. Somehow, I survived. I swapped my alcoholic craziness for a lifetime of gifted experiences. What you are about to read are a few of my experiences, some good and some bad, however all lessons, as I continue my walk toward a greater understanding of "self." Or should I say, a greater understanding of the loving energy of God.

I know that some of what I share may step on the toes of your belief system. I understand that. This book is not an attempt to change your beliefs, but rather an endeavor for me to better understand mine as I continue to work at discarding my ego-based system allowing spirit to replace it with a better one.

This is a book of my thoughts and experiences converted into the language of words. I do not claim to have the answers. As Dr. Robert Merkle, in the 1980's, used to say before each of his classes, "Remember, everything I say may be wrong." I say the same thing to you. What I share with you is my journey of experiences, strengths, and hopes.

May our journeys one day cross.

Blessings,
Jim Moeller
Maria Stein, Ohio
May 2006

A Starting Point

It was December 1980. I had been invited to the home of my then-wife and young sons.

I had been asked to move out of my home a year or two earlier because of my drinking and the actions that accompanied the drinking.

Often on holidays, I was included in the get-togethers, helping to provide a sense of stability for our sons.

Also invited were Carl and Connie, my brother-in-law and sister-in-law. By then Carl had been sober for a couple years, and I had not had a drink in nearly nine months. In the past, a day like this would have been a perfect excuse to "drink in excess," but now it had become a day of sitting and talking.

After the great meal, Carl asked me if I wanted to take a walk. I agreed, but would have declined if I knew what was coming.

Walking no farther than the short retaining wall separating us from the neighbor, Carl sat down on the wall and said, "Jim, we need to talk."

"Sure. What do you want to talk about?"

"Jim, you haven't had a drink since March, right?"

"Right."

"Are you happy with your life?"

"Sure. Life is great."

I lied and Carl knew it as he dug deeper.

"Are you sure?"

"Well, if Linda would allow me back into the house, things would be a lot better."

What I really wanted to scream was, "Everything is Linda's fault!"

"Anything else?" Carl asked.

"Things would be better if I could find a good job."

Carl pelted me with questions as he tightened the noose around my "life is great" lie.

"Jim, are you working a healthy 12-Step program?"

"Hey, I'm not drinking. What more do you want?" However, as I said this, I was thinking that these 12-Steps don't work.

"Linda says that when you're around, your anger is almost as bad as it was before you quit drinking."

It was true.

"What do you expect?" I said. "She's in the house with the kids, and I'm out here all alone."

"Back to the 12-Step program. Are you working the steps?"

"I must be. I'm not drinking."

"Not drinking is the first thing you do. To continue 'not drinking,' you need to look at yourself and deal with your issues. If you don't, you'll soon be drinking again."

Carl paused.

"Jim, if you aren't going to work the 12-Step program, you need to get other help, like treatment in a treatment center."

"Hey, I've got to get a job."

"Jim, it doesn't look like you have any peace of mind. Soon you'll find a rationalization, like Linda not letting you come back, or just about anything else, to again drink. And if you start drinking again, you may not make it back."

We bantered back and forth, and every excuse I could think of Carl had a response to shut it down.

"You need a job? You'll lose it if you start drinking again."

"Your health insurance won't cover treatment? We

talked to them and they will cover 100% of it."

"Your boys need you? Not the way you're acting, they don't need you."

"You think it is too long of a wait to get into the treatment center? They will have an opening in just a few days."

I finally gave up and accepted that every problem I could invent, Carl had a solution.

As I reflect back, it is the first time I ever gave in to a power greater than I.

In early January 1981, I drove to Wickenburg, Arizona, to take residence in what used to be a dude ranch called The Meadows.

After walking in the front door, I was met by a nurse who checked me in, did a few medical checks, and covered the rules of the house.

"Jim, I understand you drove to The Meadows."

"That's correct."

"In that case, you need to give me your car keys."

"Why?"

"Policy. We don't want you to take a late night drive after a tough day."

"Oh, okay."

"Oh, by the way, if you have a second key hidden somewhere on the car, it won't do you any good. Our maintenance people will be removing your car battery."

After she completed a few more items on her checklist, she called for one of the patients to guide me to my room.

As I got up the nurse said, "Jim, one more thing. While you're here we're going to introduce you to someone you have never met."

"Who is that?" I asked.

"Yourself."

We're Not Responsible

Have you ever felt like a parent who has failed? Do you ever wonder where you went wrong in raising the kids? I sure have. I have two grown sons, and when they were both young, I quit drinking.

Oh, it wasn't quite as simple as that. Let me say it in a more expanded format:

-My drinking caused my wife to ask me to move out.

-My drinking caused me to be a horrible parent.

-My drinking caused my wife to divorce me.

-My final year of drinking was spent living in a one-room apartment with the only furniture being a mattress and a small black and white TV, both on the floor.

It was only after all of these things had occurred that I finally quit drinking.

As time went on, I received countless hours of support from a 12-Step group, but continued to struggle with parenting. My greatest fear being that my earlier actions were going to cause long-term problems for my sons. In the 12-Step program, they talked about just working the steps and not worrying about how my sons would turn out. They said it very clearly, "Keep coming back and don't drink. God will take care of the kids."

Years later Dr. Merkle said something so unusual that the class almost fell off their chairs: "You are not responsible for making your kids turn out right." He smiled knowingly as he watched us all straighten our backs, wrinkle our foreheads, cross our arms and legs, while sending a signal of doubt his way.

He then repeated it and completed the entire statement. "You are not responsible for making your kids turn out right, but you are responsible for making yourself turn out right."

He explained that all kids come to crossroads with no guarantee which way they will go. If they have only known love, they may still opt for the opposite. If all they have ever known is hate, they may still opt for love. However, his belief was that when a child comes to the crossroad, more times than not they will follow the path that they witnessed the most.

Recently Pastor Dan said it another way: "For you parents, it is never between you and them. It is always between you and God."

Each was saying that successful parenting has more to do with working on "self" than working on the kids.

My oldest son, now a father himself, said the same thing by describing the vertical and the horizontal. Vertical is between God and us. Horizontal is between others and us. He also said, "The horizontal can never work unless the vertical is done first."

Focusing on Image and Likeness

There is no quicker way to bring another's "image and likeness of God" into focus than to give them praise.

Be Optimistic No Matter How Bad the Day

Do you want to feel optimistic on days of struggle? Jesus said that *each of us* would be able to do even more than him!

That's pretty heavy stuff, but if one is Christian and believes that Jesus was honest, then one cannot disregard those words.

Imagine, even on days that nothing is going right, there is hope. And where does the hope come from? I suspect it comes from a faith that there is a power, a loving energy, that is always at our disposal.

I feel better just letting that thought surround me.

Walk With God

When it comes to another's struggle, I have the potential to be helpful. I just have to have a willingness of the mind and body. When it comes to struggles of one's heart, I think they must take that walk with God.

Shirley

Recently a friend of mine from Ohio died. No, I didn't socialize with her when I was younger; I just knew her and her husband because we grew up in the same community.

Over ten years ago the doctors pronounced that she had cancer and told her, "Your prognosis is not good."

As in any small town, everyone soon knew of her condition and what this diagnosis might mean. However, no one knew the strength of her heart and soul.

We reconnected when she came to **Serenity** to buy music in support of her fight. Where others shied away from discussing her cancer, I wanted to know more. She talked about the cancer going into remission and then returning without warning. She described it as something always lurking in the darkness just around the corner.

Yes, we all lose friends to cancer, but Shirley was different. In spite of the toll the disease was taking on her body, she remained faithful to her God, her family, and her friends. In between the pain was a smile, and in between the fear was overwhelming gratitude for what she had.

When we talked, I told her that in spite of all she had been through, she seemed so energized. I asked her how she did that.

Her answer was simple, but her words could have a far-reaching effect on all of us if we choose to incorporate them into our daily lives: "Jim, every minute of pity is a moment lost."

She did not lose many moments.

Hitchhiking

Have you ever hitchhiked? When I was younger, I often did. Decades ago it was considered a normal way to get from here to there and back again. No one ever thought much about the risk factors.

Because of my business, I spend time both in Ohio and California. When on the west coast, I reside in the mountain town of Lytle Creek, California, and it has become commonplace for me to pick up hitchhikers either going up or down our seven mile hill. In fact, I have been given the name, "Green Car Man" by some of the hitchhikers.

One young man always travels with his guitar, sometimes playing as we go up or down the hill.

Often I pick up a schizophrenic homeless man who spends his days traveling from here to there and back again. Sometimes I join in his conversations. Sometimes he just talks to himself for the whole trip.

Another regular is a middle-aged man, originally from England. For years, he has been panning for gold in the Lytle Creek area. Whenever the heavy rains hit, his panning gear usually ends up a mile or two down the creek. When he rounds up all of it, he gets it to the road and waits for someone to haul him and his gear back up the hill. I don't know if he has ever had any luck.

Many of these hitchhikers do so because they are unable to afford a car, and if they wish to leave or return to our town, it's done with the thumb extended. Offering the rides, no matter the risk, has been the right decision because each rider has provided me with a glimpse into their life of survival.

One moonless night I was traveling up the hill almost hitting one of the hitchhikers standing next to the road. With my heart racing, I stopped the car and waited for the hiker to catch up to my car. He did not use the passenger door, opening the rear door right behind me. I jumped and without a seatbelt my head would have hit the ceiling! Nevertheless, before I could say one word, in jumped three dogs and the person I had almost hit.

What I have just described is a common type of hitchhiking, but there is another. Dr. Merkle used to say that God puts people in our lives so that we can hitchhike with them to further our spiritual path. They will teach what we need to learn at that particular moment. Then without warning, they will depart, heading in a different direction and forcing us to again extend our fictitious thumb as we await our next teacher.

Each day I need to be conscious that God is putting people in my life for me to hitchhike with. Although harder to accept, there are people that cross my path that need me to offer them a spiritual ride. If so, then I need to be prepared to journey to that most holy place where giving help and receiving help are the same.

Fact or Fiction? Just Perception

As I write this I can look toward our local landmark, Mount Baldy. Nearly two miles high, it can often be seen for over a hundred miles. Today it glistens as the snow reflects its calming purity.

My town, Lytle Creek, is situated a ridge or two east of Mount Baldy and a mile lower in altitude. What created enough snow for a million snowmen on this majestic mountain delivered more than thirty inches of rain to our lower altitude town in a five-day period. Just imagine, thirty inches of rain covering every square inch of all this mountainous ground! When the ground is saturated, where does it all go? In our area, the water rolls down the mountains first into our creek, feeding into a larger river, and eventually the ocean.

Describing what happens to this much water, as I did in one sentence, would be comparable to describing the Bible as just an old book.

During our deluge, the power and telephones continued to work until several poles finally went down as the water level increased. With no power and no telephones, I became increasingly upset as my ego demanded they fix this problem ***now***! Right now!

I was sure these mega-companies were sitting on their dead butts doing nothing while we sat in the mountains suffering.

Years ago I remember a teacher saying, "Each of our ego-thoughts leads to a perception, but perception is seldom truth." This time I knew he was wrong as my perception of these two companies was surely fact! They did not care what we were going through, they just wanted their payment each month.

Locals know there is a harrowing back way out of Lytle Creek. Unpaved and deeply rutted, this road is an artistic work of nature. As it twists and turns, one might think they will meet themselves coming and going. It is not a road for the faint of heart even in good weather!

Early one morning word quickly spread that the main road, now washed out, could be closed for up to a week or two. However, it may be possible for those of us with four-wheel drive vehicles to make it out the back way. We were also advised that if we made it out, getting back in would be impossible.

With the mega-companies doing nothing, I decided it was time to make the four-mile back road trek off the mountain.

The person who said the drive would be difficult did not exaggerate. The first mile was nothing but gigantic ruts created by the days of rain and runoff. I squeezed the steering wheel as if I would fall through the floor if I let go. Every turn brought a new sense of adventure as the drive allowed little leeway for any mistake or loss of traction.

Then another turn and all my misguided perceptions of these mega-company changed. Coming up the same hill that I was descending was a convoy of tractors and trucks, each dragging lengthy power poles around the same hairpin turns that were unsafe for my car. As they pulled and tugged, the front wheels of the tractors bounced while the drivers fought to keep the vehicle pointed up the treacherous hill.

Roads that were almost too narrow for my vehicle were now crowded with men and women using their brakes and rear booms to manipulate these poles around each turn. Often the front wheels of the tractors hung over the ravine as the driver used the leverage of the pole and boom to spin the tractor into a desired direction as they crept up the mountain.

One driver, wearing a tattered ball cap and chewing on a cigar, looked like poetry in motion as he worked the brakes and clutch with his feet while both hands worked the boom.

What I witnessed was anything but a group of people sitting on their butts doing nothing. Each driver's stamina and ingenuity was measured by the progress of their hillside climb. I used to be a military jet pilot who lived on aircraft carriers, and I can safely say that landing aboard a carrier in the dark of night was much safer than what they were doing!

Why would they take such drastic measures? Often I'm critical of large companies and their lack of integrity. However, buried within most of these companies are good people with good intentions and a strong willingness to do their job to the best of their abilities. In this case, their willingness included a risk of life so we could have electricity and telephones.

I share this story to show how I can allow my runaway ego to take control of my life. "Each of our ego-thoughts lead to a perception, but perception is seldom truth."

May God Be With You

"May God be with you."

How often have you been told that? Some of the old-timers will remember a comedian by the name of Red Skelton whose weekly TV show always ended with the words, "God Bless."

I sneezed one day at Starbucks and three people said, "God bless you."

Are these truly prayer requests of God to bless us? Will God remain dormant and then respond because I sneezed and someone suggested that God get into motion?

Here's a thought. Maybe the terms involving "God bless" aren't as much of a prayer as they are a gentle reminder. I know that when someone says to me, "God bless," I feel a sense of peace come over me. Is the peace coming from God because of the request, or is it coming because I have been reminded that God's loving energy is there for me at all times and I have allowed it in?

Congress

It is holiday recess so Congress is not creating any new laws. In reality, we could do without most of what Congress does if we, as individuals, would just start treating other people with kindness and as fellow Children of God.

I Didn't Make it to Church Today

Our weather in California is known for being mild and the envy of many, but as I write this we have just experienced another major storm that has brought more rain, rain, rain, and rain.

When I left for church I was not certain that I would be able to make the seven mile journey out of the mountains. Millions of years of mountain water run-off into Lytle Creek has dictated the twists and turns in our road. In weather conditions such as these, the water level is often higher than the road.

Maneuvering around the numerous rockslides that blocked parts of the road, I continued the descent until I met a fire truck. The driver opened the window and told me that making it through the overflow water at Long Bridge (our most troublesome spot during bad weather) was all but impossible.

As he suggested, I turned around and started back up the mountain, stopping several times to take pictures of the creek that was anything but a creek.

After stopping again, a pickup truck pulled up next to me and the driver said, "Hey, if you want some great pictures, you ought to go to Long Bridge. The water shooting over the road is incredible!"

Not knowing that God had just used this person to plant a seed, I turned the car around and headed back down the hill to the Bridge.

Having taken pictures all of my life, I couldn't wait to see what Mother Nature was up to! I was not disappointed as she provided a show that was unbelievable!

Parking about 50 yards from the "water show," I

was able to shoot pictures as I tried to capture the fury of the water.

Within moments, everything changed! Two people, an adult and child, ignoring the strength of the water, lost their footing and were swept in. Without thinking, I threw the camera down on the car seat and raced to the edge of the water where they had gone in. By then the ice cold water of the creek had taken control of their destiny and was continuing to move them farther down the hill. I could do nothing but run along the creek offering the pair moral support.

The young boy, looking at me repeatedly screamed, "Help me! I'm going to die!"

I yelled back, "You aren't going to die! You need to grab hold of something!"

"I'm going to die! Please help me!"

The boy's screams continued as the pair reached to grasp at anything solid as the water spun them in circles with its harsh freezing currents.

"Help me! I don't want to die!"

Trying not to let his words sink in, I jumped onto and over boulders that bordered the overflowed creek.

God, please help me. Please help me! I know I can help them, but I need your help!

Several hundred yards down the hill, the water took them in the direction of a large boulder, slowing their movement.

Maybe now, I thought as I quickly entered the water hoping to get a physical grip on them while not losing my own footing.

What do I do if I fall? The current is so strong!

But before I could reach them, the water ripped them away and again sent them down the river.

I fought to get back to the shore and again started running to try to catch up.

God I'm cold! And the weight of the water drenched in my clothes made running almost impossible.

"Try to grab something!"

Their yells were starting to diminish as hypothermia from the ice cold water was starting to reveal their ultimate fate.

My legs and arms are getting numb! God, help them!

The young boy was no longer pleading. Nature's power had taken away all of his hope for survival. Both were now totally dependent on the water that surrounded them.

God, help them!

A moment or two later something snagged the pair and slowed their forward movement. This was my one chance to make my way into the water to reach them. As I started to wade into the rushing water I could again feel the freezing temperature attacking my legs. I could also feel the strong currents as they tugged at me in hopes of knocking me over. I fought the water as I worked my way, step by step, toward the two. Closing in, the young boy stared at me with helpless, empty eyes. His voice was now silent as I grabbed his shirt pulling him to the shore. Once there, I went back to retrieve the adult.

By the time I pulled them out of the water, additional help arrived at the water's edge. Together, we got the pair back to the boy's hysterical mother and into my car to start warming them, and me, up.

By now the young boy's voice returned and his words changed from terminal fear to shouts of gratitude. "You saved my life, you saved my life! Oh God, thank you. You saved my life."

As I look back, one could argue that God used the driver of the pickup truck to get me there. Believe me, there is no better way to move me than to say there is a great photo opportunity! Yes, I believe God uses all of us all the time. We just need to listen! Could I have said "no?" Absolutely! It's called "free will." If so, what would have been the outcome today? I don't know. Maybe someone else would have been listening.

Do I listen all the time? Absolutely not. Anyone who knows me would agree that I have "selective spiritual deafness" as my earthly mind battles with my Spiritual Maker. Maybe some of you have the same disease and can relate to what I said.

The morning started out with my attempting to go to church, a place where I can go to join with others in giving gratitude and praise. It is also a place that helps me charge my spiritual batteries for the coming week.

So when I arrived home, frozen to the bone, I wrapped myself in a warm blanket and quietly had my own church service that centered on giving gratitude and praise while I sat in my favorite chair shivering.

I didn't make it to church that day, but I did get to witness God at work.

Quietness

Since I live alone, it is conceivable that on some days, unless customers call, I go the whole day without talking to anyone.

Sometimes this "quietness" is truly a blessing, and on other days it is most disturbing.

Why the difference?

Maybe I'm wrong, but I believe that God's loving energy is only available in the "now."

Likewise, thoughts that are not loving are normally connected with yesterday's resentments or tomorrow's fear.

So on those days when I sense a disturbing "quietness," I will probably find myself struggling with yesterday or tomorrow.

In addition, on that occasional day when I decide to "live in the now," I'm sure I'll find God somewhere close by.

Emptiness

When I live in the "resentment of yesterday," or the "fear of tomorrow," I am living in a world away from "now." Most people will agree that the love and energy of God resides only in the "now."

If I am living away from the "now," then I am living away from God and in ego's world of "illusion."

Kathy

I doubt if a day passes that we do not cross paths with someone or something that has the potential to modify our lives.

Dr. Merkle talked of these numerous potentials being brought to fruition only when we "hitchhike" with that opportunity for a period of time. By doing so, we learn what we need to learn and then we can move on.

Then there are others, a select few, who come into our lives and literally change it forever. They may be a teacher, friend, relative, or possibly someone we have never met.

I, like you, have a short list of people who have brought more to me than can ever be put in words.

One of these people is a most unlikely woman. She has never written a book or graduated from a prestigious school. In fact, she has not graduated from any school!

She and I have never had a lengthy conversation, nor argued about politics or baseball.

However, when I carried the Olympic Torch on its journey to Los Angeles for the 1984 Olympic Games, I did so in her name.

When we completed the album, ***When It's Time for Letting Go, Volume 1***, she was one of the people to whom the album was dedicated.

Who is this unique person? Her name is Kathy, and Kathy is mentally retarded.

What makes Kathy special is that she has never met a person who she could not cheer up. She has never met a person who she could not make laugh. A moment or two with her changes the focus from problems to what is really important.

One evening I was with her at the beach as the sun started to set. She stopped everything she was doing, and while staring in the direction of the sun, waved nonstop as she repeatedly said, "Good bye!"

As I watched, I saw a person who fully understood that all of God's gifts, including the sun, would be back tomorrow.

Everyone who has met Kathy knows that she will never measure up academically. However, these same people know that she is spiritually far superior having captured the essence of the "now," that place where God resides.

Over the years, I've concluded that God is love.

After being around Kathy I have concluded that Kathy is also love.

As you make your way through the day, be alert to those moments which can change your life. They may come from a sermon by a gifted theologian or the writings of a talented author or the outcome of a painful experience.

Or they may come from a person who has a special need who will have the unique ability in reshaping one's heart.

The Family Calendar

I just finished a whole day's project that included scanning, printing, and collating nearly 30 calendars.

No, these are not commercial calendars found in the store. These are much more, telling a silent story of my parents, brothers, sisters, and all of our families.

Starting each January, our family begins to take pictures that will make their way into next year's calendar.

In the "monthly" part of the calendar, we add birthdays and anniversaries. The back page is a compilation of addresses, telephone numbers, and e-mail addresses.

Although a great family tool, it is so much more—bringing together special moments and memories.

As I scan the pictures into the computer, I can't help but look at each of them and reminisce. How could I not look at pictures of my young twin nephews and remember back as they lay in intensive care barely over a pound each? How can I not look back at my youngest son and think of the moments I wondered if he would ever get through high school? Now towering over me, he is a gifted high school teacher whom students continually seek out for advice. How can I not look at my older son, his wife, and my grandchildren, and not wonder where all the time has gone?

I also included several pictures of Dad. No, they weren't taken this last year like most of the other pictures. He died a couple years ago. I can't help but continue to grieve, but then I wonder what mom thinks when she sees these pictures of Dad after spending 60 years together.

What kinds of memories will we have if we allow our work to be the center of our life?

What kinds of memories will we have if we put everything before our families?

For you see, this calendar expresses one more important thing: for each of us there will come a day that our only possession will be the memories that reside in our mind. We decide the value of that possession based on how we spend our most valuable time today.

The Glowing Embers

This morning I read a story at the ***Mountain Wings*** web site. I had to laugh because I originally heard this story, with a slight twist, at least ten years ago. Let me share it with you as I originally heard it.

There was this "old-timer" in a 12-Step meeting (an "old-timer" is a person with many years of sobriety) who was watching over this "newcomer" by spending time with him before and after each meeting, answering questions, offering advice when appropriate, and most importantly "offering fellowship."

Over time the "newcomer" started missing meetings and finally no longer showed up. The "old-timer" knew what this would eventually lead to, so he made a point of dropping in on him at his house. Invited in and offered a chair in front of the brightly-burning fireplace, they both sat quietly as they stared at the glowing embers.

Finally the "old-timer," without a word, got up and walked to the fireplace. Using one of the fireplace tools, he lifted one of the brightly-burning embers, separating it from the main fire. He then returned to his seat without saying anything.

For a short time, the segregated ember continued to burn brightly. Then, little by little, the flame started to flicker before going out. Then the orange glow started to diminish as well.

The two continued to sit and stare quietly. Finally the "old-timer" again approached the fire and moved the cooled ember back into the flames. Within seconds, the ember was again glowing and burning as brightly as it had been earlier.

They again sat quietly until the "old-timer" got up and started for the door. Finally, the "newcomer" broke the ice. "I understand. I'll be at the meeting tomorrow night."

Health and Prayer

In recent years as many of us were discovering the value of natural remedies, for generations a little lady in St. Wendelin, Ohio, had already been growing her own herbs and suggesting nutrients and homeopathy for healing.

For many she was the front line of their medical program, while others sought her out when conventional medicine failed.

When she died, many of us who had received help from her attended the service in her small Catholic Church.

While talking to the church custodian after the service, I started to learn the real truth of this unique woman's success. As we talked about her long list of accomplishments, he asked me if I wanted to go on a short tour to learn even more.

He took me inside the church, which was only a few hundred yards from the health food store that she had founded. He finally stopped next to a certain pew pointing to the kneeling bench.

"What?" I asked.

"Look at the bench."

"What am I supposed to see?"

"Look closer. This is her seat and kneeling bench. It has been hers for as long as anyone can remember.

But look closer at the bench."

I did.

"Notice that the rubber cushion is worn through and look how it is worn down into the wood. Her knees did that."

I reached down with the faith of a doubting Thomas, to touch the imprints. "They must be worn a quarter of an inch into the wood."

"At least."

As we stood there he continued to talk about her.

"Some years ago we had to start locking the church at night because of break-ins. We knew what this would do to her, so we gave her a key to the front door."

"Why?" I asked.

"Well, you have to understand this woman. We have several people in this small community that go to mass each day, but she attends the church numerous times each day, and at all hours.

"Let me tell you what I mean. After a snowfall I'm usually here by 5 a.m. to make sure all the snow is shoveled and plowed before mass. Most times when I arrive, there will be small, fresh footprints leading to and away from church. I know they are hers."

"Amazing!"

It was later I was told more of the story.

According to friends and family, she would meet with clients throughout the day at the health food store. After her recommendations they would leave, but she did not forget them. Often she would then walk to the church to pray for the person she had just worked with. She might do this several times a day.

If she awoke during the night and one of her customers came to mind, she would again walk over to the church, no matter what the weather.

What a unique concept, combining holistic medicine with God.

Someone asked at her funeral if anyone had any idea how many people she helped during her 50 years of practice. I know they were asking for a number, but let me answer it another way. Since she incorporated prayer, I would suspect she helped them all.

Let Me Have the Faith

No matter what our problems are today, let us have the faith that there is a loving energy of God available to help us at this moment.

Traffic Jam

I've found that the quickest way to be in a traffic jam is to leave the house late for an appointment.

In reality, the traffic jam was already there and my lack of preparation is what causes the problem.

Life is a lot like that. When I am least prepared to face a problem is when I am most likely to be confronted with that problem.

Be Still

On my wall I have the psalm that asks us to be still and know that I am God.

Maybe I could paraphrase it a bit and say, "Be still and allow God's loving energy to make itself known."

In my case, I should probably say, "If I can stop my monkey brain, I will be able to see God's loving guidance in my life."

Stillness. The path to God.

The Miracle of Ice

It is wintertime in Ohio where my company, **Serenity**, is located. We are a hardy group and cold weather, although complained about, is accepted. Snow? Sometimes quite deep, but we can deal with that.

However, there is a weather condition that sends fear through the hearts of all Midwesterners: ice!

The last two days have been just that. Bordering on freezing, the raindrops immediately turn into their crystal format after they collide with their earthly destination.

There are many reasons why ice is worse than snow, or snow and cold. It is the loss of control over it. We Midwesterners like to have control!

Send the cold and we will turn up the thermostat a bit. Send the snow and we will get the snow blowers and shovels out of the garage. But send ice and watch us crumble.

Ice makes the trees and power lines heavy as it tests their strength. Local residents collectively hold their breath while watching the ongoing battle between man-made items and nature. Sometimes the power lines and trees win. Sometimes they lose. Last night the trees and power lines lost.

With lost power goes the potential to heat, and for many, to cook. Still worse, because of the recent rainstorms, basements will start to allow water to rise out of the sump pump hole. Without electricity, the pump cannot empty the rising water from the lowest point in the foundation.

In California at the time, I talked to Mom several times during the storm and it was clear that she was very worried. The power had flickered many times, turning all of the digital clocks into blinking nightmares.

In spite of my telling her not to worry and giving her all kinds of spiritual reasons to turn it over to God, she was concerned! She was not alone. Many of her neighbors are senior citizens, and many have lost their spouses also.

Then at two a.m. the miracle took place! No, it wasn't that the storm miraculously went away. In fact, it was the opposite as they lost the electrical power that they so much depended upon. The miracle was that the neighbor, a farmer, knocked on the door to awaken her because he knew what would happen to the basement without electricity.

In no time at all, the neighbor had a generator rigged up and now provided mom and another of her neighbors enough power to run their sump pumps.

This type of miracle often happens in our Ohio area. It is the discovery that "God has given me a gift and it can be shared with others" whether it be a snow-plow to open up everyone's driveway, a generator when the power company goes down, or a phone call to see if someone needs something.

You see, we all possess the potential miracle of "giving." God has uniquely placed it there for us to use whenever we choose. On the other side, our "ego," the enemy of the "miracle," does everything it can to prevent us from allowing the "miracle" to flow.

How do we get unhooked from "ego" and attached with the "miracle?" Simple. Just choose differently.

The hardest part of choosing differently? It must be done in each moment.

Brother and Sister

I think most of us would do just about anything for our brothers and sisters. Right?

Since we all have the same Maker, that makes all of us brothers and sisters.

Am I doing as much as I can for my brothers and sisters?

A Thought

Everything we choose to do gets its start in a single thought.

Imagine what the world could become if each of these single thoughts were also positive.

Writing

Those of us who like to write will take an idea that can probably be expressed in a few words and expand it into paragraphs, pages, or books.

Many of the books are written to help find our purpose in life, and most of us spend our entire life trying to answer that one question.

Maybe I'm being simplistic, but I think we all have the same single purpose in life—"to be loving."

Tsunami

The day after Christmas 2004 the world was shocked into reality with the 9.0 earthquake followed by a tsunami that drastically modified numerous countries for generations to come. Unless one had business in that part of the world, there was little reason to know much about the area of Asia affected. In fact, most would have to search a bit, even on a world globe, to find it.

Today we all know about that part of the world and we all have been reminded how fragile life can be, how interconnected we all are.

Each religion has its own words for this, but the bottom line is the same: we are *all* part of a bigger picture and we are *all* an important part of that picture. Each of us brings something unique that the world desperately needs.

The same could be said about our body. Each part is beautifully interconnected and each part is dependent upon another part to remain in a healthy balance. With even small changes, the entire body could die.

Right now, the part of the world affected can be compared to an injury to our body. Imagine what our injured knee would think if it sends a signal to the brain saying *send help I have been injured*, and a reply comes back saying *sorry you are on your own.* Fortunately, our body does not do that. If there is a need, each part of our body rallies around to support the injured part.

On the lighter side, what would one think if our nose had an itch and the hand said "*sorry, you figure it out!*"

Why do I say this? Our world is injured right now

and it needs every bit of help it can get. Each of these World Citizens is part of our Universal Body. Each injured cell needs a boost from the outside to help them back to normal.

Just as when our body responds, no one is asking for extreme measures. The injured area of the world is just asking each of us to give a little bit of our excess. If we do, we will see that the world will heal quicker than we ever imagined.

Choices

I get to talk to many people during the course of a day. Many of the calls are from stores ordering music to resell, and some are from people who are at their wits' end. Something painful may have happened in their life, and they are looking to the music for additional support.

It doesn't take long to differentiate between those searching for a path to get well and others who have made a career of remaining stuck.

Many share their stories, describing a world that is cruel and hateful as they beg for pity. Most, though, know there are brighter days ahead and their faith will provide them the stability until such days arrive.

In the lives of each is a choice: To live in the painful past, fearful future, or in the hopeful present. It is always our choice.

Let me share a great example of this. There was a set of twins, horribly abused by their parents when they were young. Both grew up with exactly the same set of circumstances, but the eventual outcome was amazingly different. One became very productive and succeeded at everything he did. The other twin was nothing short of a failure at everything he touched.

When asked about their past, and its affect on their current life, their responses said it all. The one twin said the abuse literally destroyed him. He felt like a failure at everything and blamed his parents for all of his failures. He could not go a day without expressing his anger towards them.

When the successful twin responded to the same

questions, he said that the abuse toughened him. It made him stronger and more determined than ever to succeed.

Identical circumstances, different choices.

One thing is certain: we can't do anything about what has already happened. However, we can choose how we look at that past and how we deal with what arrives at our doorstep today.

Wonderful World of Jesus. Or is It?

When I attend my church, I listen to Pastor Dan as he talks about the wonderful world of Jesus.

So what is so wonderful about it?

Never being a person of instant acceptance, I usually look at what people say from various angles and then base my perception (remember, perception is what feels right to me, but is not necessarily fact) on what I have found.

So, back to Jesus. He didn't really have a job. Many people had little or no respect for him. We have all heard about his close friends who abandoned him in his darkest hour. Large blocks of people wanted to kill him.

Having said that, why has Jesus become such an influential person in my life? Forgetting all the confusing religious lingo that ultimately has belittled Him, I'm most influenced by Jesus because I don't see where he ever felt it was "about Him."

God's Energy

God's energy is always there to help. We just need to make ourselves ready to tap into it.

In the Middle of all My Books

At any given time, I am in the middle of reading five to ten books. But don't think that I am a reader who can scan a book and move onto another within a few minutes. I am one of the slowest readers in the world!

I recently read ***Your Best Life Now***, by Joel Osteen. It may be one of the most "positive-thinking" books I have ever read.

I am an "underliner" and "column writer," so I seldom loan my books to anyone. This is the most underlined book that I have ever read!

For example, one chapter deals with our thoughts and words and their effect on us. I think we would all agree that negative thought begets negative, and positive thought begets positive.

I want to share something taken from ***Your Best Life Now,*** but written by the Apostle Paul. See if it rings as true for you as it did with me. "...whatever things are true, whatever things are noble, whatever things are just, whatever things are pure, whatever things are lovely, whatever things are of good report, if there is any virtue and if there is anything praiseworthy—meditate on those things."

That two thousand year-old thought could certainly change the world!

Not Proud Of

I have done many things in my life of which I am not proud.

Sure, if I had it to do over again, knowing what I know today, I would have acted differently. I wouldn't have chosen alcohol over my children. I wouldn't have driven under the influence nearly every night. I would have spent more time with my family versus long nights in the bar.

These decisions were mistakes and I will have to live with them for the remainder of my life.

On the other hand, in the world of God, a mistake can instantly be reversed. This is most times referred to as the *forgiveness by God.*

For me, forgiveness is more of a reversal in my thinking. In doing so I turn my head away from the *ego driven negative energy* and focus on the *positive energy of God.*

Is it possible that *spiritual forgiveness* is the same as my decision to choose differently? That choice will re-connect me to the loving energy of God. Maybe *recon-nect* is the wrong word since it implies that the energy of God was disconnected from me, which never was. Maybe I should have said, *rediscover the loving energy of God* which was always there for me.

Maybe a Biblical example will help. It is the story of the Prodigal Son who was a young man who chose *things* over *spirit.* A young man who chose *ego* over *love.*

Finally, after hitting bottom, he chose differently and returned home. Without penalty and without con-ditions, his father's love was there to greet him.

The energy of God works much the same way. It is available to each of us, no matter how horrible our past and with no conditions. All we have to do is think differently to recognize the awaiting love.

Lent

Today is the first day of Lent. Officially that means Christians from around the world have entered a season of penance, soul searching, and reflection. It is also known as the season where we try to imitate Jesus and his 40-day journey into the wilderness.

As a child, I viewed this quite differently. It was 40 days without candy and little or no TV. Then as I got a little older, I also qualified for fasting as well! As you can see, each item meant the giving up of something. Needless to say, Lent was not my favorite time of the year!

If there was one positive of the Lenten season, it was the miraculous appearance of the Easter Bunny to help us catch up on the many weeks of lost candy.

Then in adulthood, I heard priests and ministers again talk of such things as abstinence, penance, and reflection. It was childhood revisited with TV and candy replaced by possibilities that are more adult.

Finally, a few years ago I went to a Lenten service to kick off the season. Pastor Mike compared New Year's with Lent and talked of the act of making resolutions. He suggested that few resolutions were successful because they only addressed half of the issue, i.e. giving up something.

He then brought Jesus into the picture by suggesting that he did not go into the desert for 40 days to give up something like smoking, overeating, or TV. Jesus went into the desert to gain something. That something was a closer relationship with God.

With silence and prayer, He was able to look at his humanness and shed it as he continued toward his destiny.

Pastor Mike then pointed his sermon back at us by suggesting that the act of giving up something just to give it up may be a mistake. He suggested that maybe we should give up something with the intention of replacing it with something more profound.

With his statement, a lifetime of confusion was corrected.

Therefore, here I am, a half century later, deciding what I will do for Lent. This year I am going to work in two areas. First, I am going to find something more productive than TV, realizing that its primary function is to provide constant noise so I don't have to face the sometimes-painful stillness in my life.

I just heard an interview with Anne Graham Lotz, daughter of Billy Graham. She said she avoided stillness in her life by creating chaos. That chaos cost her two marriages and years of pure hell.

She and I both agree that it is in the stillness that we can become closer to God.

The other area of my life that borders on insanity is diet. Living alone has allowed me to eat what I want and when I want with little or no discipline. When someone asks me if I'm getting enough of "this or that" in my diet, I seldom know.

I asked a friend who is knowledgeable in diet and health to help me create a daily menu that is healthier than my current method. She asked many questions as she tried to determine what would be best. Again, I'm not just giving up bad food—I'm replacing bad with something better.

Therefore, I've made the big circle. Instead of giving up TV, as I did at age seven, I have replaced TV with the many books I never seem to have time to complete. In addition, instead of giving up candy as I did when I was young, I'm replacing questionable food (such as my favorite of bologna on jelly bread) with healthier food.

What am I doing for Lent? I'm not giving up something, but rather, "this is what I would like to gain this Lenten season and to get it I will set this aside."

Happy or Pleasurable New Year

Do you really want a Happy New Year or do you want a Pleasurable New Year?

Most of us get them confused.

The difference? Pleasure feels good, but it is not long lasting. Like in my drinking days, the beer gave me some pleasure, but soon the desired pleasure would fade away leaving problems in its place.

Happy, on the other hand, does not sway in the wind. It is constant and always dependable.

I think the loving energy of God is like that. Supportive, constant, and dependable.

Therefore, as I write this, it is the beginning of another new year. Now it is up to me if I will be seeking a pleasure-filled year or seeking a year that has the dependability of being God-filled.

Don't Have it Together

God surely knows that I don't have it all together, and that if I try to do it alone I will never get it together. On the other hand, with others' support of me, and me of them, we can all have it together.

Giving Blood

I just returned home from giving blood. Just like clockwork, I do my best to show up, as do many others, every 56 days.

As I looked around the hospital gym, where we were all gathered, I noticed something that was most unusual: the number of young people around 18 years old were everywhere! Some wore their hat sideways with hair hardly fitting underneath. Others had so many rings penetrating their faces that it seemingly made it hard to eat! Several young males wore pants so low that their belt was about halfway between their knees and waist. My perception? A very unlikely group for blood donation.

As I lay on the cot, I asked the attending nurse about all the young kids. She told me that their age group was by far the fastest growing group of blood donors!

A second eye-opening moment took place after I completed giving blood. As usual I was sitting at the table having the required juice and snack (in my case that means numerous cookies and a couple donuts if they are available), when a volunteer walked up and asked if any of us needed anything. After she walked away, I commented to the person sitting next to me that she sure looked a lot like the other volunteer.

The person next to me laughed before responding, "You don't know them do you?"

I said, "No, I don't."

"Well, I retired from this hospital last summer and they were both volunteering here when I started working 17 years ago."

Then the shocker.

"Do you see the woman who served us?"

"Yes."

"She's 75."

"Wow. That's fantastic!"

"See the other one?"

"Yes."

"That's her mother."

Seldom at a loss for words, I could not speak.

Change My Patterns

I am determined to change my pattern of thinking this coming year.

Most believe that every thought we have is the seed that leads to something else. I agree.

Every positive thought increases my energy level and feeds into my ability to be helpful to the world in general.

Every negative thought zaps me of my available energy. It also prevents me from tapping into the universal source of all energy, God.

Negative reduces and positive increases. The choice is mine.

Maybe the Reverse is Also True

A thought as we enter Easter Weekend.

Is it not true that if we have God, we have everything?

Maybe the reverse is also true. If we feel like we are missing something in our lives, maybe it is God.

World Need

I need to become more conscious of the real needs of the world. If the needs of the world are greater than mine, then I need to help.

The Alarm Clock

Some years ago I went on a retreat that was hosted by the Benedictine Monks in Southern Indiana. The topic of the weekend retreat was "gratitude."

A fellow retreatant spoke up and said that remembering to give gratitude was the toughest part. He confessed that he would just get too busy to remember. An elderly Monk listened and then reached into his pocket and pulled out a watch that was on a chain. Although it looked as old as he, it was a modern watch with an alarm clock function.

He explained that when he traveled, the watch would provide for him what the bells did when he was here at the Abbey. He went on to say, "Our bells provide you with chimes each hour to tell you what time it is, but more importantly, they provide you with a reminder that another hour has passed." He then said, "Another hour that God has blessed us. Another hour that we have the opportunity for giving gratitude."

He was right. However, I went back to my business life forgetting the valuable tool he had offered. It was several years later that I heard the chimes of a set of bells that brought me back to the moment with the elderly Monk. Instinctively, I stopped what I was doing, looked at the bell tower, and gave thanks for the previous hour.

This time I did not let that moment slip away. I tried all kinds of things on my computer to get it to beep at me each hour. Unfortunately, with all the amazing things my computer could do, it refused to be told to make some kind of hourly noise.

Finally, after spending several hours trying to get one of my software programs to do what I wanted, I found the solution! A $4.99 digital clock was sitting right in front of me and its alarm function could be changed to the next hour within seconds.

Now, being in business, I could not control when the telephone would ring. I also realized that asking my customers to hold a moment while I gave thanks for the previous hour was not going to make good business sense.

Then, there it was again. It was like the person who invented this little travel alarm knew just what I was thinking! The inventor had added one more feature that was perfect for my situation: a snooze alarm! Now when the alarm goes off and I am in the middle of a telephone call, I just hit the snooze alarm and it will keep reminding me every few minutes.

After a few weeks of this, I incorporated something else. If you are like me, you probably own several daily readers. I own more than several. In fact, I own at least 30 of them. I now have several of my daily readers on my desk, and each hour after the alarm clock goes off, I grab the next book in the row to absorb what it has to offer. No, I gave up a long time ago reading the daily reader on the day it is supposed to be read.

What has been the outcome? I am shocked how much better I feel throughout the day! Did it make any of the problems go away? No, but it has better prepared me to deal with them in a positive manner.

Then there are other calls where the caller has come to **Serenity** because they are struggling with an issue and they are hoping our music might help. The hourly reminders, followed by the readings, have helped me to be ready to offer the spiritual support that is necessary.

That little alarm clock reminds me each hour to give thanks for all that has been given to me. It reminds me that each hour is precious and suggests that "I look at what I have done during the last hour and has any of it made the world a bit better?" Oh yes, besides the reminder to give "thanks" and the "reminder to do another small reading," the alarm clock also has another function. It reminds me that I have put wash in the washer or wet clothes in the dryer versus my discovering it days later. As you can see, I am truly grateful for this $4.99 gadget.

Ending Lent

Today is the day before Easter and the sun is yet to rise as I complete my morning readings. Some six weeks ago I turned the TV off and replaced it with something more valuable and rewarding: reading books focusing on spirituality.

With Lent coming to an end, I found myself staring at the books I have been reading and was shocked when I realized that many of them are quite old.

I don't know about you, but I am one of those people that look at the inside of a book cover to see when it was published. If it is new, it may provide me with all the answers I am looking for. If it is a few years old, it is probably of little value or I would have heard of it. I suspect it has something to do with "the answers being magically out there somewhere" versus "you already have the answers, just go inward and tap into them." Little by little I am realizing that the older the book, the more wisdom it probably contains.

In the last hour, I have been reading from several books. Let me share some of the words with you.

"I want volunteers…who will pledge themselves... for one year not to do anything without first asking the question, 'What would Jesus do?'" WWJD. I have seen that four-letter icon numerous times in the last several years. A great 21st Century thought? No, it came from a book, ***In His Steps*** written by Charles Sheldon and published in 1897.

In another book these words jumped out at me:

-"Many areas of knowledge have little to do with

the soul."

-"If his head contained all the knowledge in the world and yet his soul was empty of all charity..."

-"Everything is vanity except loving God."

-"The eye is never satisfied by what it sees, nor the ears by what it hears."

-"Certainly better is the humble farmer who serves God than the proud philosopher who entertains thoughts about the heavens."

Powerful words. Which best selling author wrote them? Thomas Kempis. You haven't seen his name on the *New York Times* bestseller list? He wrote them in a book called ***Imitation of Christ*** that first hit the market in 1429. No, that is not a typo. Well over 500 years ago.

Another quote: "Everything you can comprehend through faith's vision belongs to you. Look as far as you can, for it is all yours." These words are in today's reading from L.B. Cowen's ***Streams in the Desert*** written in 1925.

"The way to deeper knowledge of God is through the lonely valleys..." taken from A.W. Tozer's book, ***The Pursuit of God,*** written on an all night train ride in 1948.

"Whether our prayer is private or public, it is the same spirit praying in us...touching different strings on the same instrument." Thomas Merton, a Trappist Monk, wrote that in 1950.

"The name of God is the name of nothing and of all things." I'll have to reflect on that statement a bit. It came from James O'Conner in his book, ***Silent Fire, Bringing the Spirituality of Silence to Everyday Life***.

I am also reading from Joseph Girzone's book, ***Joshua In A Troubled World,*** that brings Jesus (known as Joshua) to a post 9-11 Washington, DC. An interesting book.

Each of the listed quotes was read in less than an hour and that was a typical day of readings during Lent.

To think I could have turned on the TV and instead of reading these life-changing words, I could have watched a rerun of "Gilligan's Island."

How Many Meetings?

I continue to work with people involved in a 12-Step program. Most of them come to me by telephone not knowing of my 12-Step connection. When they call, they are doing so because of our music. In the course of the conversation, something usually is said that leads to a discussion about the grip that alcohol had on the caller.

One young man, not too enthusiastic about going to many meetings, commented. "I don't like going to all these meetings that people tell me I should go to, but the judge ordered me to. They all use the term that I should keep coming back. How long do *I need* to keep coming back?"

We talked a little bit longer, and then I asked him if he really wanted to solve his problems with drinking.

"Sure I do."

I then responded. "You asked, how long do you *need* to keep coming back?"

"Yah, how long?"

"Until you *want* to keep coming back."

It is then that one knows that there has been a transformation.

More Than Basketball

More Than Basketball, Vol. 1
More Than Basketball, Vol. 2 and
More Than Basketball, Vol. 3

Each essay was written about a week apart and since they refer to each other, I left them together.

More Than Basketball, Vol. 1

Recently I went to a high school basketball game to watch my sister's son who has now grown into a 6 foot 5 inch center. The game was more than exciting with both teams demonstrating why they have made it as far as they have in the statewide tournament. My nephew's team won and they will continue in the tournament.

In the stands cheering for the same team was a husband and wife carrying more pain than one could ever put into words. Their son, a close friend to every member of the basketball team, died just over a month earlier.

They tried to be supportive, but with each joyous moment, their pain could only grow. I am sure they could not understand how their friends and neighbors could be so happy while they carried so much pain in their hearts. To them it must have looked like everyone in this small town had forgotten their son as they resumed their normal life.

Since this was the final game for the District

Championship, each member of the winning team received a medal. Then basketball tradition sent each member of the winning team up a stepladder to cut down part of the net. These pieces of cloth would provide each member a lifetime memory of this high school achievement.

After each member of the team had secured a piece of the net, the seniors went back to the ladder to jointly cut off another piece. Then, without hesitation, the group walked off the court and ascended the bleachers with no one knowing why they were doing this.

After climbing the five or six rows, they stopped directly in front of the grieving parents and presented them with a piece of net. I can assure you that anyone who witnessed this moment was truly moved as the tears flowed from everyone's eyes.

In spite of all the joy this win represented, these young men did not forget how much the dead teenager had meant to them during his short life. In the middle of the cheers, they chose a higher path by giving something back to this struggling family.

If the majority of teenagers are like these basketball players, then our future is safe. What they exhibited is so eloquently described by the author of ***The Pilgrim's Progress***, John Bunyan: "You have not lived today until you have done something for someone who can never pay you back."

More Than Basketball, Vol. 2

Last night it was back for more basketball. My nephew's team followed up their district championship with a win earlier in the week at the regional level. This was now the regional finals, and at the end of the night there would only be four schools of this size remaining in the tournament for the State of Ohio.

Fans knew the previous tournament games had all been tough, but this game would be in a league by itself. The scouting report said the opposing team would run like deer and play much of their game above rim. Their 20+ wins were not accidental!

By now the actions taken by seniors a week earlier were well known by every basketball fan in the surrounding community. Their gesture of presenting part of the net to this grieving couple epitomized the thoughts of all the local people. One person told me, "I often think of them and the pain they must be going through, but I just don't know what to tell them. I also miss their son."

The gesture by these young men opened the door for those apprehensive people to come forward and share what was in their hearts. Many just held the couple and cried. Others grabbed their hands to give them any extra strength they could offer. Each found a way of expressing their love to the grieving parents.

The game followed the scouting report. The opponents were fast and they could certainly jump, doing all the things that good basketball teams must do. At times, it looked like the game would slip away. Their speed was causing our team to commit numerous fouls, while passes were often intercepted before they reached their target.

However, the team hung in as they played with an intensity of knowing they were playing for more than themselves. Little by little they closed the gap and finally took the lead. Somehow, our passes now seemed to find a path that our eyes could not see. Our shots, blocked earlier, made it over the extended arms of the opposition and landed in the basket.

Unbelievably, our team started to pull away from what many believed was a superior team. When the final buzzer sounded, the opposing team stood there in disbelief having been beaten by a dozen points.

The players must have thought they were dreaming as a caravan of reporters and TV cameras descended upon them. Then, just like the previous week, the step-ladder was brought on the court to cut down the net. With each cut they were reminded that they truly had made the final four and would make a once-in-a-lifetime visit to play on the court of The Ohio State Buckeyes in the State Championship.

In reflection, the team played as if they had an unfair advantage. During the second half, their movements and passes were dictated as if they had seen a video tape of the future and knew just what to do. To an observer, like me, it looked as if their shots and passes were being guided by an invisible sixth man.

The net was now down. The cheering was starting to subside from the hoarse fans while the tournament officials were starting to herd the boys into a group for official pictures. Most of us know that teenagers seldom listen to authority and these kids were no different. Without warning the seniors left the group and headed to the bleachers, just as they had done a week earlier. With TV and still cameras in the chase the seniors again reached the grieving couple and presented them with a part of a net that would now become a matching set on the mother's blouse surrounding her son's picture.

I talked to the couple earlier in the week and they could hardly express how important this gesture had been. I reminded them that the players "giving" gesture would never have happened if they had not been "receivers." I repeated that for every act of love there is a "giver" and a "receiver." It was their willingness to face all the internal pain and still go to the game that made all of this possible. I know that it would have been a whole lot easier for them a week earlier to stay at home in an attempt to hide from a pain that continued to stalk them.

As a person who has lived with the 12-Steps of a recovery program, I know we need to live one day at a time; however, for those grieving, one day is an eternity. With raw pain they have no choice but to live a life of putting "just one foot in front of the next." The boys helped the parents take one more step toward a healing that must seem a million miles away. These boys were giving back to the parents the same love that their son had given to each of them throughout his life.

My personal belief is that no gesture of love ever ends. It just continues touching all that comes into its path for the rest of time.

We are in the Easter season and all Christians

know the resurrection ultimately means there is "no death." The grieving parents, over time, will come to know that is true. Last night was an example of that as their son, unseen to our human eyes, lived fully in the hearts of the players as they gave us more than we ever expected. Yes, their son lives as he and his basketball friends continue to teach us "old" people what life is truly all about.

More Than Basketball, Vol. 3

The high school basketball season ended for my nephew and his team last night, but not before we were treated to one of the most exciting games I have ever watched.

With our team having a 1-point lead, we watched an opposing player throw up a "Hail Mary" shot as he was falling out of bounds. It went through the basket as the gun sounded.

In just a couple short weeks I was able to watch some young men give us a snapshot view of what life "is about" and what life "can be about."

Let me explain. If we want to risk greatness, then we must get out of the boat and trust that God will be able to support us as we fight to stay afloat on the treacherous water. I learned it another way: It may be risky to step out of the boat, but it may be more risky to sit there and do nothing. These kids took the step even when some of their early season critics said that winning half of their games would be a lofty goal.

I recently read that to accomplish anything one must first plant the seeds. No matter how much praying a farmer does, he or she will only reap the rewards of a harvest after the seeds have been planted. If you want to be a doctor, you must first plant the seeds of medical school. If you want to be a successful basketball team, you must first plant the seeds of practice, practice, and more practice.

Then, if you want to be spiritually successful, you must have the faith that giving part of the harvest away will be the planted seeds for the future. These boys did all of those things. They prepared with years of seed planting as they honed their skills, and when others said they were destined for mediocrity, they stepped out of the boat and put their faith in a power greater than themselves.

They then took their success to the next level. As the crowd celebrated their District and Regional titles they took their winnings, their harvest, and gave that precious moment to a family struggling so painfully in grief.

The season is now over. Did they lose? The newspaper box score says "yes," but I think not. The only possible losers will be those of us who don't follow their example.

Past, Present, Future

Past, present, and future. Books and books have been written about it.

The "present" is the momentary link between the past and future.

The "present" is the ground I currently stand on. I can stare toward the direction I'm going and know there is a "future." I can turn around and look at the footprints of where I just came from, the "past."

As I spin around, I can look behind or forward. As I do, I am free to make any decision I choose; but that decision must be made from the spot where I am currently standing, the "now," not where I'm going or where I've been.

Business

When one is self-employed there is always a fear of what tomorrow may or may not bring. As much as I try to avoid that fear, it lingers. I've concluded that I have a long way to go to get beyond the fear. I just have to be cautious that I do not allow the fear to cause me to quit.

All Things Work for the Good

Today the sun has taken the temperature above freezing. When this occurs there is anticipation that spring is just around the corner. When you live in a farming community, one's daily routine is centered around the weather.

Starting in childhood, I watched the farmers, including my grandparents, depend totally on God for their livelihood. Some years the rain would be too heavy and other years it was not enough. My grandfather never complained. He just gave thanks for whatever came each day. He would say very simply, "I know that God knows more of what's going on than I do."

What he was saying was a slightly modified version of the Biblical saying, "All things work for the good for those who trust in God." His statement, along with the Biblical one, has stuck with me. However, that does not mean that I readily accept it. On days when things are not working out the way I want, the "All things work for the good…" sneaks into my mind. I wonder how many times my parents and ex-wife had to say (and wondered if it were true), "All things work for the good…" while I was terrorizing the world with my alcoholic behavior.

In the last year I have received more calls than ever before from people struggling with personal, family, and health issues. Although I do believe that eventually "All things work for the good…" how could I tell that to someone who has just had a loss in their life?

One day I received a call from a man whose son

had died in an auto accident. Someone had suggested our album, "***When It's Time for Letting Go and Letting God.***" I listened as he talked of his life's focus on work instead of his son, and now he felt overwhelming guilt. His son was gone and there was nothing he could do to undo his commitment to work. "All things work for the good...," but I knew there was no way I could discuss this, and I'm not sure I believed it myself.

I thought about him for a couple days and wondered how I would react if I were in his shoes.

Soon after, an elderly woman from Georgia called to place her first order. Within a few sentences, I knew this woman was totally at peace. She wanted a recommendation for a family member who had Alzheimer's. In the course of our conversation she spoke of several other family members who were terminal or very sick, including her husband.

After her comment about "feeling so blessed" I asked her how that was possible with so much sickness in her family. Without hesitation, she said these so-called problems had ultimately become opportunities. She continued, "Young man, if you read the Bible then you know that 'All things work for the good for those who trust in God!'"

For a moment I was speechless. I then asked her how that could possibly be. How can things like death work for the good? She continued with the faith of a minister. "Son, let me help you understand that verse on a day-to-day basis. 'For those who trust in God, nothing of love is wasted. Nothing. No experience. No occurrence. No gesture. Nothing is wasted if it is given with love.'"

She brought it into perspective. Does it remove the pain of loss? Absolutely not, but it did help me to look at it differently.

The next day I sent a note to the man I had talked to days earlier. I told him about the telephone call and I told him what the lady had said. I then said to him, "All the good things your son ever did were never wasted. None of it. Everything done with love would continue living and affecting all that it would touch." I asked him to consider how his life was already changing because of his son's love.

The bottom line? Nothing that happens to us is ever wasted, including those things that cause great pain, because "All things work for the good for those who trust in God."

Dad

Last night I went to a function that included a lot of old friends. Many of these people I would not have ever met had it not been for our kids being involved in sports. With the kids now grown, all of us would agree that we don't see each other enough anymore.

The reason we met was to do our drafting for what is called a baseball rotisserie. What that really means is that a bunch of us get together and each selects a fantasy baseball team that competes with the selections of the other guys.

In reality, it is nothing more than an excuse to get together in a much too busy world to fellowship with each other.

At the end of the evening, I spent time with two men I have known for nearly 20 years. Both of them talked about the declining health of their fathers and how physically and emotionally difficult it has been.

As they talked, I could not help but reflect on my father's declining health before he died. They talked of wishing that their fathers would attempt to do more and be more active as they had done all of their lives.

I remember arguing with Dad, trying to get him to change his eating and exercise habits to counter his diabetes and heart disease. The more I pushed, the more he resisted and I found myself getting visibly angry at a man who was doing nothing more than getting old.

In frustration I asked for help and received some great advice from a friend. "Jim, there comes a moment in life that the only thing you can do for your parents is just love them." I thought about that numerous times. This friend was right.

From the moment of acceptance, I no longer felt the need to change Dad back to what he had been. I found that I was okay with where he was at now. With this new view, I could enjoy my time with him versus the frustration of my inability to change him.

In those moments of helping instead of changing, I could return the love and gratitude for all he had done for me in my life. No longer was there an expectation, just gratitude.

Did that make the pain of current and future losses go away? No, but it did make each moment more of a celebration as I looked at his broken body as a testament to all the good he had done.

The fathers of both my friends are also good men having spent lifetimes helping others, but with failing health that has ended. On the surface that was true, but looking deeper it was far from accurate. Experience has led me to believe that when love is given, it perpetuates for all time, going from generation to generation.

In this case, that love given from my friends' fathers to them had been cemented into the sons with the unbreakable strength of DNA. So, in spite of the parents worn out bodies, their love still shines brightly through their sons because, as I believe, love never dies.

The Rudder

Last night as I was reading I came across this metaphor that is found in the Bible. The story compared the rudder of the ship to one's tongue, while comparing the ship to a human being.

Although the ship is infinitely larger than the rudder, the ship will go wherever the rudder guides it.

We are the same way. Our body is far larger than our tongue, but the words we use will guide our actions and determine our direction.

Dedicate My Energy To

In this coming year, what will I dedicate my energy toward? I know a certain amount will go toward my work. Another block, unfortunately, is eaten up by sleep.

What about the remaining hours? If the first thing that comes to mind is not the enrichment of my relationship with family and friends, along with my willingness to help others, then the God-given potential energy will be wasted.

Hate?

Have you ever been around someone who doesn't like anyone, is critical of everything, and is just plain negative in general?

Most therapists would say that this person does not like himself or herself and they project it on everything around them.

Look around. Republicans dislike Democrats. Democrats dislike Republicans. Independents dislike both parties. Yes, these elected leaders when referring to their counterparts often use the word *hate.*

Why is that? Would the psychological rule still apply when a therapist suggests that they actually dislike themselves? Probably. In addition, dislike of another is a byproduct of one not getting his/her own way. Ask any parent how many times their children have told them they hate them? At that moment, the children (or the congressional representative acting as one) are not getting their way and they are upset because of it.

Dislike of self or one not getting their way is the goal of ego. What is ego? Ego is everything that is not God, not loving.

I learned long ago that anything that separates us from others makes us less. When a basketball team no longer plays as a team, they will fail no matter how many points the superstar scores.

We split the term God into various religions and each categorically says that their religious God is the only true God.

Congress is split with an aisle. One is either on the "right" or the "left."

There are countries with artificial boundaries that constitute countries, states, counties, towns, or personal property. Often the only way to determine the boundary is with surveying equipment. However, people are willing to die over artificial boundaries.

Each time we separate, we become more distant from God, the encompassor of all, and more attached to the ego of what is not love.

Here is a novel idea that has been suggested a few billion times: Accept the belief system of others without shoving our belief system down their throats. Accept each other no matter what country they are from, or what religion they believe. Accept them as children of God.

Here is an idea that probably won't happen this century: When our congressional representatives arrive in their chamber, they draw a number each day and whatever number they draw, that is where they sit for that day. I'm willing to bet that as people get to know each other they will start to understand each other. Then, maybe, words like dislike and hate will start to disappear.

Idealistic? Of course.

Diversity

Recently I went to several high school girls basketball games in Ohio that included the small high school I attended (created havoc in) some 40 years ago.

Our community may be small (my high school class was 66 students and it has not grown much since then), but it boasts one of the most successful academic and athletic programs in the state. It is a testament to the individual taxpayers in this community that know the importance of good education and ethics.

In this game were several girls from our small town who will be playing college basketball somewhere after they graduate. As they performed, I could easily see the teamwork that had evolved from good coaching and commitment to be the best.

One of the girls was relentless on defense causing the opposing team to make mistake after mistake. If the opposing team let down their guard for even a second, the ball would be stolen. However, I never saw the opposing team give up. As the game intensified, I watched each movement be countered by an opposite movement followed by another strategy change. It was like a chess game on a basketball court.

As I watched the opposing team do their best against this above-average player, I took a journey into my past.

I was a very gifted athlete in high school and had the potential to play several sports at a much higher level. One of the schools we played had a relentless player who had the same tenacity of the young woman I was watching. His name was Jan Bachman and he literally drove me crazy as he guarded me. His feet moved so fast that his tennis shoes never stopped squeaking. Over and over his hands reached in as he attempted to steal the ball. And steal the ball he did.

After stealing the ball from me for the third time, he headed down the court toward his own basket. I reacted. I ran after him and tackled him! Remember, this is basketball, not football. A fight nearly started as I was sent to the bench for the rest of the game.

The bottom-line? I was faced with a challenge and instead of reaching deeper, I chose a different and unfair path.

During the recent girls' game I saw it differently. As the defensive person worked nonstop to steal the ball, the offensive person worked even harder to prevent it. In other words, the diversity caused by one person was causing the other person to become an even better player. I had done just the opposite.

We are all faced with challenges each day that are metaphorically asking us to choose between reaching deeper, no matter the pain, or just giving up.

Memorial Day

It is Memorial Day today. Most of us know it as the holiday that unofficially kicks off the summer.

As a military pilot during the Vietnam era, I view the day differently. All across our country today there are parents who choke on their tears as they grieve the loss of their sons and daughters.

However, as they experience their lifelong "loss" they can relish the fact that their "infinite donation" has brought freedom to each of us.

Memorial Day is both a "day of memories" and a "day of giving." Take a moment to reflect on the loss suffered by these families and then give thanks for their willingness to give so much. Blend both their "loss and their gift" and allow that feeling to reach the core of your soul as you enjoy your "blessings of freedom."

Look around you. Would you be willing to give all of your freedom away? If not, then join me as I send a prayer of gratitude to all the families who have given so very much.

Follow on Note:

In two weeks it will again be Memorial Day, a year since I first wrote this "Reflection." Recently the war came closer to home when friends of mine, Lou and Linda, lost their son, Bryan, in a helicopter crash in Afghanistan. Bryan was 24 and on his third overseas tour.

When he enlisted I sent Lou an email thanking

both him and his wife for their willingness to share their son in the continuance of our freedoms. Now Lou and Linda, as well as Bryan's wife, Kati, Bryan's brother Scott, have given their ultimate sacrifice for that freedom.

As time passes, may they find comfort in knowing that all we hold sacred will remain that way because of people like Bryan.

A Simple Thought

I probably have over 500 books on my shelves and each attempt to define the "ins and outs" of life in a unique way. This morning I received one of those motivational emails that travels around the world going from computer to computer, entitled ***Old Farmers Advice***. Here are a few lines from that email:

"The biggest troublemaker you'll probably ever have to deal with watches you from the mirror every mornin'."

"Always drink upstream from the herd."

"Good judgment comes from experience, and a lotta that comes from bad judgment."

The last item on the ***Old Farmers Advice*** list probably says more than any book I own:

"Love generously. Care deeply. Speak kindly. Leave the rest to God..."

Imagine what would happen to the world if we did just that.

In the Now

There is nothing that I work harder on than trying to "live in the now." At the same time, there is nothing I fail at more than "living in the now." It is almost impossible to not worry about the unseen tomorrow or yesterday's decisions as I try to survive in an ever-changing world.

I have this endless argument with myself as I try to make business plans that deal with the future while trying to "live in the now."

Today I was given a most unusual gift that helped bring me back to the "present moment." As I do most days, I went jogging in the mountains. While huffing and puffing, my mind was preoccupied with the work we are doing on several new albums. Struggling with the financial side that accompany new projects, I was fearful if the album would be accepted in this economy.

Then I tossed out a half-hearted prayer, "God, what should I do? Money is tight and I…" No sooner had I completed the question when a blue jay started its shrill whistle from 50 or 60 feet away. Instantly my focus went to the bird as I tried to keep an eye on it as I ran. It jumped from one bush to another, almost as if it were following my path.

Finally I stopped and just stared as the bird continued to sing its off-key song.

Then, just as quickly as it arrived, it departed.

After a few moments I again started to jog when I realized that this blue feathered critter had done for me what I could not do for myself. The chirping helped to quiet my mind, helping me to come to the "now," and then teach me that God lovingly walks (and even jogs) with me in each "moment."

Use Me

"God, I want to be used to do more. Please use me to do more." I have repeated this prayer for as many years as I can remember. The components, I am certain, were introduced to me somewhere in my childhood.

"God, I want to be used to do more. Please use me to do more." Although not always obvious, in the course of my workday this prayer was being answered. Owning a small music label that creates relaxation music to help support people's healing, I may talk to as many as 50 people a day. Many of these callers did not seek us for entertainment, coming instead to find support with the psychological or physical pain they were carrying.

Day after day, year after year, the prayer remained the same: "God, I want to be used to do more. Please use me to do more."

Then, without warning, the prayer took on new meaning as my brother-in-law, Carl, lay in a hospital bed waiting for an organ transplant due to a genetic illness. Carl was special. Besides being a blood relative, he was married to my ex-wife's sister, and we had known each other our entire life.

Due to the company he worked for, and for me the military, we both ended up in California living within a few miles of each other. We did many things together, including jogging, coaching baseball, and drinking. Yes, lots of drinking! Therefore, when Carl realized he had a drinking problem and chose sobriety, many of the old social events that centered around alcohol no longer took place.

Over time, my drinking followed his, and as my

life started to spin out of control, he was there to introduce me to the same 12-Step program that had become so important in his life. Our friendship then changed. We no longer spent hours drinking; we now went to 12-Step meetings and spent hours talking about a different way of life.

Just as Carl had been there for me, I wanted to return the favor to him. *God, I want to be used to do more. Please use me to do more.*

With a country as big as ours, it seemed hard to imagine that a liver would not eventually become available. In my mind, it was just a matter of time.

Days came. Days went. No donor.

God, I want to be used for more. Please use me to do more.

Another day. Another week. No donor.

I want to do more.

God, I feel so helpless.

God, where is a donor?

God I want to do more. Why can't I help?

Just because my blood type is different, why can't part of my liver be used?

A donor was never found.

As I stood in front of Carl's casket on the day of the funeral, I could only feel the personal failure of wanting to help save his life as he had helped save mine.

God, why didn't you answer, surely there had to be someone who was willing to help.

God was quiet.

Before the lid was closed on the casket, I heard myself repeat the daily prayer with a slight twist. *God, I am sorry you did not use me, but if the day ever comes that I can prevent another family from experiencing this nightmare, I will be ready.*

God remained quiet.

Several years went by and then, in early 2001, just before heading out on an early Sunday morning jog, I had a fleeting thought that I should buy a newspaper on the way back. Seldom buying a paper, I tried to push the thought out of my mind.

When the thought would not subside, I gave in by putting several quarters in my pocket before heading into the mountains for a long run.

As expected, the newspaper was more than an inch or two thick, filled with layers and layers of word-filled nothingness. Arriving at the last insert, the ***Parade*** section, I almost tossed it before deciding to scan it. There it was—a story about organ transplants with the theme centered on how a few people, non-relatives, were starting to emerge as living donors for people they had never met. New anti-rejection drugs had continued to improve and someone who would have died a few years earlier could now survive a transplant from less-than-perfect matches.

As I read the story, memories of the helplessness I felt as Carl slipped away were rekindled. As I read the story, I mentally revisited every word of the silent prayer I had offered in front of the casket: "God, please use me, and if the day ever comes that I can help another family..."

I left the newspaper article on my desk for several days, not certain what I should do, but knowing something would come of it.

By the end of the week, I reread the article several

times. With no plan, I finally called the University of Southern California Medical Center, knowing it to be a prestigious school. After a few telephone transfers, I reached a person who knew all the answers. Even a few that I did not want to hear.

I explained that I had called to inquire about their living donor program, and before I could ask any additional questions, I had already been disqualified as a liver donor because of my age and my history of alcoholism.

I felt my heart drop, as if they had pronounced a death sentence to my prayer.

Then the doctor continued, "Even though you do not qualify as a liver donor, there is a chance that you could qualify as a kidney donor."

The doctor reiterated that due to anti-rejection drugs, recipients no longer had to have that nearly-perfect-match that only family members could offer.

After a burst of questions and telephone calls, the idea of being a donor was starting to become a reality. The telephone rang nearly every day as I received calls from either the doctors or the staff members as they continued to delve into my personal health, as well as my motives for becoming an organ donor.

Then, without warning, USC became very distant, no longer calling and seldom returning calls initiated by me. I was later told that this was their way of allowing me to reconsider the decision I was contemplating.

Finally, as if they rediscovered a lost file, I was asked to come in to the hospital on numerous occasions to determine if I would be a quality donor. I had no idea there were so many physical tests and so many psychological questions that could be asked.

Besides all the normal tests that included various things stuck into unusual places, I spent hours, on one occasion, periodically drinking a beverage that resembled orange pop from my childhood. Tasting similar, it was densely packed with some form of sugar that was then measured as my body processed it. On another occasion, just before they slid me into a tube for some form of imaging, they told me they were going to give me an injection that would give my body symptoms similar to a woman having hot flashes. He did not lie! My body felt as if the tube they slid me into was actually a microwave oven in disguise and they had set it on *high*!

Psychologists and psychiatrists asked me questions until they could not think of any more. I learned later they were trying to determine if I was doing this to help another, or if I was dealing with guilt from my past.

After nearly a year of waiting and testing, I received a telephone call from Toni, the USC coordinator for this program. Kiddingly, she said, "Jim, you passed. You graduated. You are considered to be donor material."

Responding to her comment, I asked, "You mean, like in school, I passed? Will we have a ceremony like with cap and gown?"

She laughed, but quickly moved to a more serious note asking, "Jim, are you still okay with this? If you are, we can start looking for a match."

A match, I thought. As if to fight the fears of the path I had chosen, I answered her question with a bit of sarcasm. "Heaven help the person who would have a close match to me. Sure, if you think you can find someone, have at it."

During the next several weeks, the Medical Center worked behind the scenes to find the best possible match to assist in reducing the rejection rate.

Then on May 24, I received a call from Toni telling me that a good match had been found and she again asked, "Jim, are you okay with this? You know you can still back out."

After giving an answer that would change the lives of many, she told me that the transplant had officially been scheduled for May 29, 2002, just five days later. She then said, "Jim, this is a very serious life-and-death surgery and I must remind you that it is important that you get your personal things in order."

Without thinking I said, "Toni, I have two comments. First, I think this is more of a life-and-life surgery instead of life-and-death, and, secondly, if I live to be a hundred I will not have my life in order and now you want me to accomplish that by next Wednesday? There isn't a chance of that."

After both of us stopped laughing, I asked if I could have the person's name so I could substitute it into the prayer I had been saying since my first call to USC. Toni told me that her name was Valentina.

Valentina, I repeated it several times and then I thought to myself, what a beautiful name.

Toni then spoke, "Jim, if you are a go, the next phone call we make will be to Valentina telling her that a donor has been found."

"Call her? You mean she knows nothing about this?"

"No, we never want to build up someone's hope until it is certain. She does not even know there is a possibility for a match."

After we hung up, I sat quietly for a long time wondering what Valentina—and her family—were feeling at that moment.

God, please use me. I want to do more. Is it possible, I thought, *that God's plan really did include me as an avenue to change the course of another's life?*

On the morning of the surgery, I drove to the Medical Center, arriving so early that the guard had to let me in. As I went through the normal check-in including one more blood test, one more urine cup, and one more blood-pressure test, I couldn't help but wonder what Valentina was experiencing. I struggled to put a picture of her in my mind, not knowing if she was tall or short, married or not married, kids or no kids. All I knew was that her name was Valentina.

The rest of the day was a blur. In the haze of recovery, I can remember asking how Valentina was doing, always falling asleep before hearing the nurse's answer.

Finally, late that evening, I remained awake long enough to hear the staff's answer and, this time, I remembered it. "She is doing great. Your kidney kicked in right away."

I remembered putting my head back in the pillow saying, "Thank you God. Thank you for using me to do more."

Although I requested that I get to meet Valentina, it would not happen unless she agreed. On Friday afternoon, two days after the surgery, Toni walked in and scolded me. "Jim, I understand you have been touring the hospital stopping at the nursing stations and asking questions about a possible patient named Valentina. Is that true?"

"Yes, I just wanted to know who she was. I wouldn't have talked to her or anything. I just wanted to see who she was."

"Jim, you know you can't do that. Besides that, do you think for one minute we didn't think about you trying to find her? We changed her name at her nursing station."

She paused.

"Now, would you like to meet Valentina and her family? She agreed to meet with you."

Later that afternoon, I was taken to her room. There she was, Valentina, the recipient of the prayer, "God use me..." Nervously sitting up in bed, her long, dark hair draped over her shoulders. With a smile and tears intermixed, she was surrounded by her three young daughters, her husband, her father, and an interpreter since the adults spoke no English.

In spite of the language barrier, for the next twenty minutes we spoke in our native tongues saying things our brains could not interpret, but our hearts fully understood. We spoke the universal language of love and tears.

As I held Valentina's hand, I looked into the eyes of her family, knowing God had truly put this plan into motion years earlier as I stood in prayer at Carl's coffin.

Valentina and her family are now adjusting to a life of normalcy for the first time in years. Instead of coming to grips with the reality of an impending death,

Valentina is now back to being a vibrant mother and wife.

Although I continue to talk to the family at least once every few months, the call just before the first Christmas after the surgery is the most memorable. "Jim, this is Maria, Valentina's daughter. How are you doing?"

"I'm fine. How is your mom?"

"She is doing good. I just wanted to call for mom and see how you are doing and tell you Feliz Navidad and to thank you for giving us our mother back."

Her words were humbling and the only response I could come up with was, "You're welcome."

I would be lying if I said this has not had an impact on me as well. We have all heard words like, "what you give, you will receive," but I suspect the reverse may also be true. I have concluded that God gives each one of us an abundance of loving gifts and if we do not share these gifts, we will eventually lose them. For me one of the gifts has always been above average health and if I chose not to share the gift, I would eventually lose it.

I think of Carl often and know that his illness eventually led to the donation to Valentina. I suspect that is how life works: we learn from one and apply to another.

On weekends I still go jogging in the early morning hours often watching the sun make its way over the mountain peaks. I no longer have the choice of buying a newspaper or not because the paper machine that was so instrumental in the life of many has been removed. So when I return to my small house, I make my way to my favorite chair grabbing my homemade prayer book reciting a few of my favorite prayers. The last one continues to remain the same:

God, I want to be used for more. Please use me to do more.

Note to reader: This story was most difficult to write because of its personal nature. If you have not done so, please make your wishes known and carry an organ donor card in your billfold or purse. It will be the greatest gift you can ever give another, and yourself.

Follow the Light

Nearly every day I jog up here in the mountains surrounding my Lytle Creek home. Although I have an unlimited number of directions I can go, I tend to follow one of three routes. After hundreds and hundreds of jogs, nature continues to overwhelm me.

Recently I have been given an opportunity to watch one of nature's least respected members, weeds, as they taught one of the great lessons of life.

One of the three routes is on a paved road going on for miles. Being Federal land, there are no homes, no human beings, no nothing, except nature.

Last fall it was decided that the asphalt on the road was no longer adequate and so it was ripped up and trucked out making the road more of a gravel road variety. Due to heavy rains, it took several months for the construction company to get back in and complete their job of repaving the road.

As one would expect, after a couple months and lots of rain, the road looked more like a weed patch than a road. However, with heavy machinery the road was graded, more gravel brought in, and a 3-inch coating of asphalt applied.

Although a gigantic waste of money for its minimal usage, it was nice to have a smooth surface to run on.

Approximately a month after the paving, I noticed that the road was starting to grow little bulges. With each passing day more bumps appeared, and they were starting to grow. It didn't make any sense.

Finally, like on a day in spring when every tree pops its miniature leaves, the growing pimples of the road popped open allowing the weeds that had been graded and covered with tons of asphalt to come out.

I had never seen anything like it, and with each passing day the weeds continued to break the asphalt into small chunks.

The weeds, of all things, were providing a lesson about going to any lengths to reach the light of God.

Many books discuss the Light of God and how it becomes most visible when life becomes the toughest. These weeds showed me, by example, what those words really mean.

Accomplishment

As I look back over the previous year, I would like to think that I have accomplished quite a bit in my life, as well as in my business.

However, when I look further back, I know that I have often failed in many areas of my life, including parenting and business decisions.

However, there are times when the opposite seems to occur.

One of the toughest life-lessons for me to learn is that my accomplishments do not come from me. My accomplishments come from what God has given me. Failures come when I choose not to use the gifts that God is offering me.

What am I Thinking?

What am I thinking of at this very moment? Is it positive or is it negative? Whatever it is, that is what I am creating as my universe in this very moment. If I don't like my universe at the moment, I need to then think differently and watch my world start to change.

Salesian Monastary

I have been selling music to a Catholic Brother at the Salesian Monastary giftshop in Broadheadsville, PA, for years.

From the first call I knew that Br. Bernard and I would be life-long friends because there was something about his calls that made him different. I knew it was his spiritual quality with words that seemed so simple when compared to my life of confusion and disarray. I would get off the telephone and wish for myself to have his sense of peace.

Recently I received a note from him and inside was a plastic bookmark that now travels with each book I read.

The Order he belongs to is based on the teachings of St. Francis de Sales who, according to the bookmark, "found the secret for holiness in the ordinary actions of the day. He taught others to turn these everyday 'little' actions into opportunities to practice 'little' virtues of holiness."

On the backside of the bookmark was the key to why Br. Bernard was so at peace. As I read the bookmark I could see him in each word. Let me share them.

Seven Salesian Virtues to Make the Ordinary, Extraordinary:

1. To others little acts of selfishness and unfairness-*Endure patiently.*

2. Amid your shortcomings and limitations-*See the bright side.*

3. When others are curt with you-*Show good humor.*

4. At the tiresome tempers of others-*Stay cheerfully excusing.*

5. When someone turns you down-*Put on a good face.*

6. If someone helps, when you'd rather do it yourself-*Be appreciative.*

7. When answering others-*Speak gently and show courtesy.*

Nothing really earth shattering. Just good common sense. Then again, all loving thoughts and actions are based on nothing more than common sense.

One last line on the bookmark: "In this way, we can do ordinary deeds, extraordinarily well."

Fathers Day

Today is Father's Day. Currently in California, I called Mom in Ohio this morning and asked her if she would go to the cemetery where Dad is buried and thank him for me.

Oh, I know that the dad I remember is not residing at the cemetery, but there are times when one must return to a place of memory and build upon it for that moment.

The sermon in church this morning centered on, "It's not about me, it's about the work of God." Pastor Dan asked each of us to reflect on ourselves and see if we were "always looking for a blessing from God (all about me), or are we a blessing to others (all about the work of God)?"

What a day to ask that question. That was Dad. I can never remember him turning down anyone who needed help. If a call for volunteers went out, he was first in line. Besides his 20 years of activism with a family foundation for the neurologically impaired, he could be found every Memorial Day putting flags on numerous cemeteries in memory of the veterans. After a snowstorm, while others were asleep, he would be plowing all the sidewalks at the local church.

If any of us kids had a problem, we could call him and receive expert advice. In plain English, he was a man of common sense. He had the ability to listen to a problem and turn it into a solution. He taught me how to do electrical work, plumbing, and carpentry by telephone. When a new roof was needed on my house, he was on the roof showing me how to do it.

He was the rural letter carrier for our area, driving over sixty miles a day. Because of that daily connection with so many people, he kept an eye on the elderly as if they were his own parents.

Sure, I have a lifetime of memories, but that doesn't stop the emptiness on a day like today.

Months after his death I was channel surfing when I came across a show on the History Channel about the Army's 10th Mountain Division, his unit, as they marched across Italy in WWII. Without thinking I turned on the VCR to record the show for Dad. It was minutes later when the realization of my action hit me. Although I shut the VCR off, I continued to watch the show that described a part of his life that he seldom talked about. Numerous Purple Hearts had lain in a drawer for as long as I could remember and now I had a chance to see the combat that had caused them to be there.

Yes, Dad may be gone, but he is far from being forgotten; and, as a gift from God, Pastor Dan was able to bring him back today, Father's Day, as he described Dad's lifelong philosophy, "It's not about me."

Religious or Spiritual?

The church that I attend also has a Bible study on Wednesday nights.

After the minister completes his talk, we break into small groups to discuss the topic a bit further. Currently we are studying Acts. This section of the Bible describes many of the individuals who were around Jesus on a day-to-day basis. It goes on to describe how these people started out with the frailty of being human and over time, by being around Jesus, became spiritually transformed.

All of us would like to put ourselves in that "transformed" category. However, are we? Having always been a rebel against organized religion, I am amazed how numerous "so-called" believers miss the mark. I hear the term over and over, "I'm saved" while we step over a person in need. "I'm saved" as we cheat our fellow man. "I'm saved" as we repeat over and over, "My religion is the true one and everyone else's is wrong."

Have we been spiritually transformed or religiously brain washed?

Am I religious? I hope not. I may be wrong, but it appears to me that all religions are man-made and come with fabricated baggage. On the other hand, spirituality is God-given. I would rather accept the gifts of God versus the baggage of man.

Has our church, synagogue, or mosque helped transform us? What does our daily life most resemble? Mother Teresa? Or the "I'm saved" cry of the hypocrite.

Anyone who has to "tell you" that they are living the life of "God" is probably trying to convince themselves.

I am often reminded of a statement, "If you did not know what I was, what would you think I was?"

Two Wolves

Several years ago I heard a story describing the internal battle we all struggle with.

This weekend I heard the story again and, as the first time, the wisdom touches all of us.

A young American Indian approached his grandfather for advice. "Grandfather, there is a terrible fight going on within me. It is a fight between two wolves."

"Grandson, can you tell me about the wolves?"

"Yes, grandfather. One wolf is mean and ugly. He talks of anger, war, hate, greed, resentment, lies, and selfishness.

"The other wolf is beautiful and good. He talks of joy, peace, love, serenity, hope, kindness, fairness, compassion, and gratitude."

"Yes, grandson, you are not alone. This same fight goes on inside of every human being."

After pausing, the young boy then asked, "Which wolf will win?"

The grandfather then responded, "The wolf that you feed."

A Lesson that Keeps Coming Back

Yesterday I stopped at a frozen yogurt shop to purchase a yogurt.

Following another person into the shop, we both made our way to the counter. Other than the employee on the telephone, we were the only people in the shop.

Both of us looked over all the options as we waited on the young woman to finish her call.

Quietly we waited and waited. Finally the other customer turned and said, "Not much on service are they?"

As I prepared to respond I took a look at the woman on the telephone who just kept talking. "Yeah, it's hard to find good help, I guess."

We continued to wait.

Finally I spoke, "Do you think she would hang up if we went behind the counter and helped ourselves?"

The other customer then said, "These young people just don't understand anything about working."

Just as I was about to respond, the door flew open and in ran a police officer. The employee quickly hung up the telephone and ran to meet the officer. Yes, she had been on the phone, not with one of her friends, but with police, describing the robber!

In the middle of her description for the on-site officer, she stopped and looked at both of us. "I'm sorry I made you wait but the police on the phone wanted to know everything I could remember."

At that point the officer decreed that the shop would be closed until the investigation was complete.

The teenager then said, "I'm sorry, let me give you a coupon that will give you a free yogurt the next time you come in."

I said, "No, that's okay."

I got in the car and looked back inside the shop as she continued to give the officer valuable information. As I stared, I realized this young woman went from "she should be fired" to "she should be running the company."

Amazing how often the lesson of "perception is seldom fact" makes its way into my life.

Counselor

Years ago I was a marriage and family counselor. After working with hundreds of couples, I concluded that for a marriage to be successful it could not be a 50/50 proposition. This meant each would be willing to give half to the marriages success.

For a marriage to be truly successful, it must be a 100/100 proposition with each giving their all.

12-Step Programs discovered that decades ago when they said, "half measures avail us nothing."

Inside out, Outside in

I have to keep reminding myself that it's "inside out," not "outside in." Will I ever get it right?

Journey

We are all on a journey. We all need help. If I want to find my way on my path, I have to help you on your path.

Jogging

I often talk of jogging. This has prompted a few of you to send emails asking if I ever do anything but jog. Others want to know how I ever get anything done if I jog so much.

I had to laugh, but it did start me thinking about why I do go out and abuse my body each day. Some days I hunger for it as much as others crave a bite of chocolate.

In general, I seem to feel better when I jog and I tend to get more things done. Let me paraphrase a famous theologian when he was asked, "If you pray four hours a day, how do you ever get anything done?"

His response: "Sir, without my four hours of prayer, I would never get anything done."

The response made perfect sense to me.

Recently I read that walking, or in my case jogging, as "taking a stroll with your soul." Sometimes that stroll ends up being a mental argument as my ego and soul do battle.

Maybe I jog because it is good for my health. Certainly it is, but if that were the only reason then healthier eating would become more important.

The bottom line is this. Jogging and walking help the body, the mind, and the spirit.

As I become more disciplined in a routine of daily running, my body starts to quiet down and I become ready to let my spirit and the jogging merge. In other words, I start to feel the presence of God.

Those of you who are Christian will remember that

Jesus would often escape into the hills for prayer. I find the same escape in jogging.

I have a turnaround point on one of my scenic routes. Often I stop and just stare at the miracle of nature. Sometimes it is so quiet that I truly hear nothing. Other times, when I've worked out harder than I should have, the only thing I can hear is my heart beating. I am never closer to God than I am in that moment.

Another reason why I think jogging changes my perception is the use of affirmations while running. Positive thoughts, repeated over and over, pull me further from ego and deliver me to the "now," to the doorstep of God.

Here are a couple of affirmations that I have repeated thousands of times: "Use me to do more," "Make me an instrument of Your love," "Help me know You better," and "Your will, not mine, be done."

So why do I jog? It is my form of prayer, and I am convinced that without it I would never get anything done.

I Can't Live With Myself

I was at a 12-Step meeting last week when I heard a member state, "I finally quit drinking when 'I' just couldn't live with 'myself' any longer."

I've said the same thing many times in my life, but this time hearing someone else say it, it sounded different.

Who is 'I' and who is 'myself'? I suspect that one of them is our "loving self" and the other is our "ego self." The "loving self" is God given, inherent to all of us, always there at our disposal. On the other hand, the "ego self" is something we've created and only as powerful as we allow it to be. Only as strong as the energy we delegate to it.

Therefore, as this 12-Step member recognized, if he were to survive and stay sober, he was going to have to change something in one of the two "selfs" to dictate his future. He would either have to suppress or expand the "loving self" while dismantling or giving additional energy to the "ego self."

The choice was his and his choice would be based totally on his desire to remain sober.

We Need A Driver

I have written one sentence in my journal numerous times, "We all have a gift and we need to share that gift."

For many the gift may be obvious, but for others their gift may be obscured or unnoticed.

This morning Pastor Dan asked for help. He had received a call from a friend in Tucson who headed up an orphanage across the border in Mexico. She called in desperation with a plea for food from our church pantry for her orphanage kids. Her cupboards were bare.

Without hesitation, he committed our help.

After describing the conversation, he followed with a request. We had the food and we had the truck, but we had no driver. Without a commercially-licensed driver, the food would never leave our church.

Pastor Dan asked if there was anyone who could offer the gift of driving.

At the completion of the service, everyone started to exit. I followed behind a young woman, probably thirty, who followed behind another woman, probably her mother.

Just before we reached the door, the younger woman asked the older, "Now where did my husband go?"

They stopped in their tracks as they scoured the church looking for the missing person. Finally the older woman spoke saying, "There he is. He's up in front talking to the minister."

I turned around and looked. Pastor Dan and the

young man were in serious conversation.

"What can he be doing up there?"

All traffic had stopped as the women continued to stare at the young man.

"What can they be talking about?"

I finally spoke up asking the younger woman if her husband was a truck driver?

"Well, yes he is. Why?"

"I have a feeling he is about to take a trip to Tucson and Mexico."

"What? Him drive the truck? I don't think so. He's never done anything for anyone else in his entire life."

I don't know how this story ultimately turned out, but I suspect the minister's plea was a moment in which a young man finally realized that he, too, was blessed with a gift he could share.

Independence Day, Vol. 1

I just finished a long morning run up here in the mountains.

Today is July 4th and today, like all holidays, I take a slightly different route, jig jogging through a park and then a campground both managed by US Park Rangers.

The first leg takes me along the creek in Lytle Creek, and I wind around until I'm heading even farther uphill into the mountains.

Holidays are special days up here as thousands of people converge on the park and campground.

On the first holiday after I moved here several years ago, I was shocked when I headed out on a six a.m. run. There were already hundreds of cars parked up and down the road waiting for the park to open!

I was so shocked by this that I mentioned it to a couple of friends who had grown up in this area. Both said that families, mostly Hispanic, have been coming up here for generations. They said it had become as much a family tradition as a Christmas tree at Christmas.

In today's world as many buy more and more big outdoor toys in hopes of creating holiday fun, these generations of local families continue to rediscover what is important.

On days like today I often stop to watch, listen, and absorb the tantalizing smells that escape the hundreds of BBQs.

Kids are in and out of the snow-fed ice-cold creek

inventing games that only kids can do. Picnic tables are covered with piles of food!

Each holiday I find myself increasingly envious of all these families coming together to celebrate. They don't have dirt bikes, 4-wheelers, or expensive speed-boats. They have something much more valuable; they have each other.

From Head or Heart?

Years ago as a counselor, I would welcome new clients nearly every day. Each of them, unique in their individual problems, were universally the same in their emotional pain.

The first session was normally cut and dried as I would listen to their problems and then make an initial assessment. One of the evaluation points was the honest appraisal of my capability to help the troubled person or family.

With a large amount of training in my field, I liked to think that I could help everyone who passed through the door. At least that is what my ego was telling me.

Over time, I came to realize that what the ego was telling me was not true. There were areas where my alcoholic background made me a valuable source, and there were areas where my only knowledge came from a book.

With all of this knowledge, I knew how to identify the problem and I knew what experts said to do about it. That is treating a client from the "head," which is what most therapists do.

Then a few years ago I became a hospice volunteer and again went through training as I prepared myself to be helpful to the terminally ill person and their family. As years earlier, I learned the necessary steps I was to take if I was to be helpful.

Since then, I have been honored to work with numerous families that have experienced death. However, when I would work with them, I was transported to the days of my "book-learning therapy" and often felt inadequate to deal with their pain.

Then it changed. My dad died.

From then on I began to work with hospice and grieving clients differently than before. Talking to Mom daily, I found myself psychologically walking with her as we both addressed our pain. Pain for me, the child, was heavy but it could not compare to what she must have felt after spending 60 years with Dad.

After Dad's death, I found that my moments with hospice families changed. I could still be objective as I heard them talk of their pain, but now I knew their pain.

All of us can give advice from our "head" telling someone what they should do, what they should feel, and when they should feel it. When we deal from our "head," we can be overly callused as we tell them to get on with their life.

However, those who have experienced the death of a friend or loved one know differently. They bring something more to the grieving moment. Sure, they bring their "head" but more importantly, they bring their "heart."

Religion or Relationship

I have battled with religion for most of my life. The term religion has never felt right. I finally concluded many years ago that my hang-up about religion and God is that religion has little to do with God, being man-made to fit the conditions of the human maker. On the other hand, spirituality is God-given.

Having said that, why do I go to church? There are many reasons, but the biggest one is that my church has continued to help me understand that church is not about religion. Church is about developing a relationship with God.

Pastor Dan said it another way, "It's not about religion, it's about relationship."

Baby With Promise

On Christmas Day Pastor Dan talked about the birth of Jesus. As he said, "Jesus was a baby, just like any baby, but with promise."

We're all like that. In each moment we are who we are, but with promise.

Independence Day, Vol. 2

What do Independence Day, 60's singer Bob Dylan, and a Catholic nun have in common?

When I was growing up in our little town of Maria Stein, Ohio, we were home to a convent made up of a large number of Catholic nuns. Because of their level of education, many taught in our school even though we were a public school.

During our senior year of high school, we took an English Literature class that was taught by Sister Theona who, at that time, was close to retirement.

Throughout the year we followed the traditional curriculum writers, from Beowulf to Shakespeare. Then one Friday she announced that the following week we would be studying someone not in the textbook. She did not elaborate.

On Monday as we approached our library classroom, we were greeted with the popular music of Bob Dylan. For the rest of the week we studied the wisdom of his words and music. He was a favorite of all of us; and because of that, new life was given to the study of literature.

In 2005, nearly 40 years later, two academic books were released each elevating the writings of Bob Dylan to the same level as many of our world's great writers. Sister Theona was far ahead of her time.

Now back to my first paragraph. What do a Catholic nun, Bob Dylan, and the 4th of July have in common? As we reflect on Independence Day, let me quote Dylan's radical words of the '60s:

"I think of a hero as someone who understands the degree of responsibility that comes with freedom."

July 4th. Sure, it's about fireworks, but it is also about "reflection on the past," "gratitude to those who made such far-reaching decisions centuries ago," and, as Bob Dylan so beautifully sang, "responsibility that comes with freedom."

Víctor Hugo

Do you have certain writers who just seem to speak to you? I do. One of them is Victor Hugo. "Who" you ask? Victor, living in the early 1800's, is one of the world's most accomplished writers. Remember ***Hunchback of Notre Dame***? How about a book that became one of the most successful Broadway musicals of all time, ***Les Miserables***? Both of these he wrote.

Today I opened an email and there he was again. His words, written more than 180 years ago, "Hope is the word which God has written on the brow of every man."

"Hope." What a powerful word! Sometimes as the world continues to crazily spin, it seems that "hope" is the only thing we can hold onto.

According to Hugo, God has etched hope into each of us and that "hope" is the strength we need after we have tripped and fallen trying to just live life.

Last week Victor showed up again. I was reading a book that was helping one deal with pain. "Sorrow is a fruit. God does not allow it to grow on a branch that is too weak to bear it."

In an earlier book, I underlined his entire paragraph. As you read his words, note how each of the keywords has a psychological implication as well. "Emergencies have always been necessary to progress. It was *darkness* that produced the lamp. It was *fog* that produced the compass. It was *hunger* that drove us to exploration. And it took *depression* to teach us the real value of a job."

Dr. Merkle often said, "Pain pushes…while truth

pulls."

In those words he was suggesting that "pain" would be a teacher, whether we wanted it to be or not. He was also suggesting that "truth" could also become a teacher, and always available to us. All we had to do was be willing to grab hold of the "truth" rope and let it pull us forward.

Unfortunately, most of us have chosen to grow through the "push of pain and emergencies." It would be nice if we could choose to learn all of our lessons without pain, through truth, but we're stubborn that way.

Then again, when unwanted pain surrounds us, we always have hope to fall back on. Emily Dickinson said in one of her poems that "Hope is the thing with feathers– that perches in the soul…" The same "hope" that Hugo said God has etched into the forehead of our soul.

Just Sit and Die

I have two churches that help feed my spiritual need. One is in Ohio, the other in California. Both do one thing that continues to bring me back each week. They talk of an unconditional, all-loving, God that even I, with a lifetime of mistakes, cannot offend.

Both churches are grounded in the desire to help others. This past weekend our associate pastor started the service by asking for prayer for the members who were traveling around the world in help of others.

Pastor Dan was leading a group of more than 20 to Indonesia to see how we could expand our orphanage to better serve the tsunami victims. Another group was on the way to New Zealand. A major group was in Mexico helping to build homes. Before he finished, he listed at least 10 groups and the support they were offering.

He concluded with, "Oh, let's not forget the high school students you saw in the back of church. Tonight they are all going to be on Skid Row to serve the homeless."

By the time he concluded I found it somewhat surprising that we had anyone left in church!

My Ohio church does many of the same things, and Pastor Mike often says, "If you came here to find a comfy seat on Sunday mornings, you are at the wrong place."

Because Pastor Dan was traveling, we had a visiting minister for the sermon. After being introduced, he started out by congratulating us for being such an active church. He told us that we had a far-reaching reputation for service in helping others. We sat a little bit taller after hearing that.

He then lifted a copy of the weekly bulletin, pointing out that there were several additional needs for volunteering within the church. As he pointed to the document he said, "With your reputation you would think there would be people standing in line to volunteer."

We sunk back into our seats.

Then the visiting minister complimented us again on how we, when asked to do so, greeted all the people sitting around us.

Then he rained on our parade for the second time when he asked why we didn't take the initiative to greet each person as they entered our row, not after being asked to.

He then changed his direction explaining that he wasn't trying to be critical. He was using the two examples to springboard into his sermon about four lepers who often met at a particular gate, waiting to die.

He explained that they must have met often, but none of them ever spoke to each other. He explained that their actions were a perfect metaphor for most churches. He was certainly right!

He continued with the Bible story stating that finally, after some unknown period of time, one of the four finally spoke, saying that they needed to do something or they would just sit there and die. Only when they finally stepped out by taking action could the energy of God work through them.

He then brought us back to the "present moment" by asking us if we knew the strengths of each of the people around us. If so, how could they mesh with ours?

Asked them their strengths? I didn't even know

their names!

What he spoke of made perfect sense and caused me to speculate as he continued to speak. Looking around the church, I wondered how much "potential" energy was sitting in our church waiting to be used.

Imagine for a moment, what could be done if our church, as well as others, broke everyone into groups of four allowing each group to pool their ideas and their energy.

I'm not much of a fan of vegetables, but I love vegetable soup. Alone the vegetables are just so-so, but blend them together and they become a masterpiece!

Let me give you a personal example of a small group making a difference. In the early 1980's, living in California, I decided I wanted to give something back to the Ohio community where I grew up. I had little extra money, so if I were to give something it would have to be the "energy of service."

I made a telephone call to a Linda and Larry, friends from the past. Linda had become disabled due to childbirth complications and because of that they were on a speakerphone. I explained to them what I was hoping to do and wondered what they thought.

Suddenly an unknown voice chimed in. It was the nurse who had been attending her. "Jim, I don't mean to interrupt, but I have a suggestion." She explained that a group of people was trying to start a grass-roots center for the treatment of people with brain injuries. Their goal was to do as much of it as possible with volunteers.

I approached my parents, brothers, and sisters to see if they could assist me in this. To make a long story short, for 20 years my family pooled their collective energy to raise money for the center. Hundreds of people have been helped, keeping with the founding group's dream that no one has ever paid a penny out of their pocket for treatment.

We knew nothing special about what we stepped into. All we had was a willingness, while the other group had a dream. Their idea married with our energy.

Consider what I just described and how it may be applied in our lives. What about a call to a couple of our friends? How about the card club or the bunko group? Maybe our parents, brothers, or sisters? Neighbors? How about our various churches? In recent years, many churches have focused on small groups. This would be perfect.

Start the ball rolling by telling your targeted group that you have an idea that could change the world. What is the idea? Doesn't matter. By getting your group together, the idea will make itself known. At that point, the energy to manifest the idea will be born.

Imagine the potential outcome! If we were to all do this, I confidently promise only one thing: we will make a difference and our world will never be the same again.

Is it Conditional or Unconditional?

Have you ever heard the term "conditional love?" What about "unconditional love?" This weekend I was doing a show in which I was selling our music. I often get into discussions with customers who enjoy the music and as they listen, we start talking about all kinds of subjects.

One person I was talking to used the term "conditional love" so I asked him what the difference was between "conditional" and "unconditional" love.

He thought about it and then said, "I don't know."

Is it possible that the reason he could not find a definition is because there is no such thing as "conditional love?" I think love is either "unconditional" or it isn't love at all.

I could see that he struggled with my opinion.

For example, deep down we know we love our kids no matter what they do. That love cannot be increased or decreased. That doesn't mean we like all of their actions (or that they like ours), but not liking their actions does not mean I love them any less.

In one of Pastor Rob Bell's sermons, he talks of a child who worked hard on a project in hopes of impressing his dad with it. When dad arrives home the child comes running to show off what he has done. However, dad does not need to see what he has done. Just seeing his son is all that dad needed.

I think God must be that way. We often feel we need to do certain things and in certain ways to get God to love us. That is how many religions survive as they institute their own twists, turns, and hurdles. Maybe the bottom line is that God just loves us no matter what. That doesn't mean that our actions are always acceptable, but it does mean that the love is constant and never changing.

Somehow My Parents Got Smarter

I told my parents some years ago that the older they got the smarter they became.

My parents, through all of my drinking and craziness, remained stable, caring, and understanding. However, that did not mean that I was receptive to their compassion.

Over time, and as I started to change, I became increasingly aware of their tremendous wisdom. In other words, the older I got, the smarter they became.

Mark Twain said that "when I was a boy of fourteen my father was so ignorant I could hardly stand to have the old man around. But by the time I reached twenty-one I was astonished at how much he had learned in seven years."

I found the same thing to be true of the 12-Step program. For over a quarter of a century I've attended these meetings, and with each one I become increasingly aware of the program's wisdom. In other words, the older I get the smarter the program becomes.

Affirmation

Often I will lie in bed after I wake up and in the dark go through some affirmations. When I do so, I seem to be much more ready to face the world when I get up.

Yesterday morning I again did that. "God, help me to learn something new today." This time, before I could even think of what I was saying, I received this response, "And may you put it into action."

"Putting it into action." Yes, that is where the problem lies. Stubbornness, ignorance and a multitude of other rationalizations get in the way. Often given the gift of learning and so seldom put it into action. A 12-Step priest used to say, "yup, action is the magic word."

Run

If you find that I am trying to "change you," run!

Love is my willingness to "accept you." Ego is my desire to "change you."

As I said, if you feel that my ego is at work, run!

Mapquest

I often use a web site called Mapquest.com that allows me to put in my current address and the address of my destination. After some computer gyrations, it comes back and tells me what roads I should follow to get there.

Life is like that also. We know where we are. We know where we want to get to, and we need to determine what roads we need to follow to get there.

However, the roads suggested are often not obvious and may take me in directions that I'm fearful of going. Yet, if I want to arrive at the destination, I have to trust the process.

Years ago when I was a professional counselor, my first question was always the same. "What are you hoping to achieve by coming to see me?" People often would say that they wanted to find love in their life. That was their goal, their destination. At least they thought so.

If I want to reach a specific destination, then there is a path that needs to be followed. If the destination is love, the path to get there must be a path of being loving.

Here is the essential concept that I believe to be true. Love is not a destination. Love in one's life, I believe, is a byproduct of being loving.

If our goal, our destination, is to get even with someone, then we need to follow a path of vindictiveness. Vindictiveness is a by-product of being vindictive.

If I want a suntan, the tan becomes the byproduct of sitting in the sun.

What do I want in my life? The destination is always a reflection, a mirror, a Mapquest of the route I choose to get there.

My Limits

Who defines my limits? Whom do I blame for getting in the way of the desires of my heart? Is it society? Maybe family? Lack of money or time?

What is it that I want to do but haven't?

When I talk with friends they often say, "Jim, you have experienced so many things in your life. More than I could ever imagine." In the same moment I look at others and realize that they have done so much more than I have.

I don't know about you, but I battle daily with what I hunger to do and what I actually choose to do. What is the invisible force that is stopping me? Where is the blame for lack of accomplishment? Certainly I could create a long list of rationalizations, but that is all they would be.

The bottom line is this: The only person who can stop me from reaching my dreams is me, and the sooner I quit blaming others, the sooner I will become successful.

As the old Pogo comic strip implied, "We have met the enemy and it is me."

Help Just One

Normally I do my "daily readings" in the early morning. Then, before I sit down at my computer, I may turn the TV on to see what has happened in the world since the night before. Most of the talk this morning was about Hurricane Katrina and her sister Hurricane Rita.

Immediately I felt overwhelmed as I thought about the possible reenactment of Katrina's arrival. I knew the churning inside was due to the helplessness I was feeling. I sat down at the computer and started downloading the nightly emails with that strange sense of emptiness.

There on the screen was the answer to my anxiety. One of the downloaded emails was from BeliefNet.Com under the heading of ***Daily Inspiration***. My hero in life is Mother Teresa, and when people talk of God, they must be talking about someone like her. The quote of the day was from her: "If you can't feed a hundred people, then feed just one."

I, like probably most of you, have already donated to one of the Katrina funds. I knew this morning that original donation was not enough.

I went to the Bush-Clinton Katrina site and donated a bit more. Enough for a meal or two because I knew I could not afford to feed a hundred today, but knew I could feed one.

Where is the Wonder?

Last night I was reading a book in which a Rabbi Heschel was quoted. He stated something that I could not agree with more. "As civilization advances, the sense of wonder declines."

Each day we have the entire universe available to us, but seldom do we see it. If you are like me, you're chained to your desk and computer for a large part of the day. Even in work, what used to be meetings or one-on-one telephone conversations have been replaced by impersonal emails.

The timesaving treadmill or gym often replaces jogging with nature.

Don't get me wrong, many advances in technology have been positive and life changing. However, none of the advances can replace the healing qualities and beauty of just being aware of everything around you.

On days when my mountain jogging is a bit more painful, I may run for an hour and at its completion not remember one thing that I saw.

I need to listen to my own advice. One of my favorite statements when talking to newcomers in a 12-Step program is suggest that they "be here now." In plain English that statement suggests that you take one look at what surrounds you and become fully aware of it, all of it, in each and every second.

One of my favorite jogging routes takes me by countless wild blackberry bushes. During the blackberry season I see millions of purple berries glistening in the sun. They often replace entire meals as I stand by the bushes in my jogging gear.

Last winter I woke up to find that a snowstorm had dumped nearly a foot of snow during the night. Without hesitation my camera and I spent the entire morning looking at the "here and now" photo opportunities.

Although I am in a mountain town, most residents are unaware of the unlimited berries, and everyone I met had nothing but complaints about nature's beautiful white coat.

It is Saturday morning and as I write this I am awaiting the sunrise. Saturdays allow for a longer run and more time with nature. I won't know until I am on the trail if I am in tune with nature or the pain in my body.

Another runner suggested that on days that my body is in pain, I slow down to a pace that will still allow me to watch nature while physically challenging my body. He said that excluding nature is to exclude God. Good advice!

The sun has now risen and I am going to spend the next couple of hours with naturc. Oh, I mcan God.

New Years Day

Is it possible? A year has just ended and I was given 365 days to do all the things on my list.

What did I do? Sure, I accomplished a few things, but if I had a chance to review the 8760 hours from last year, what would I find?

I would find that for the greatest percentage of those hours I wasted my time. Much of the year was spent living, and I use that word "living" loosely, as a couch potato in front of the TV thinking about what I will do later. Maybe tomorrow. Maybe next week. Maybe sometime.

What I've concluded as I look back on the last year, is that eventually we will all end up "returning to the home of our Maker." It is up to us to decide what we do before that moment arrives.

Faith, Hope, Trust

Often I lack in faith, in hope, and in trust. Try as I might, I struggle in reestablishing each of those virtues.

Then without warning, someone comes into my life, usually a friend or family member, who jump-starts my shortcomings.

It is as if I am allowed to borrow from their abundance until my inherent seeds again start to grow.

Teachers Approach Immortality

My youngest son is a high school English teacher with a focus on writing and journalism. Because of the way similar classes are structured, many students will have my son as their teacher several times during their high school years.

One of the techniques he uses is to have the students write about "themselves" in nearly all of their assignments. For many, this brings new meaning to Socrates' statement of "know thyself."

Because he is also a baseball and wrestling coach, I often go to the events in which he is coaching. It is during these events that I am often approached by many of the parents of his students.

Repeatedly I have heard that his relentless focus on their "self discovery" continues to cause positive change in their children's lives. Many tell me their children entered my son's classes as typical teenagers and came out the other side as young adults.

All of us hope we can make a difference in the world while we are here. Nevertheless, for most of us that is just a wish.

After talking to these parents, I am certain that good teachers plant seeds of growth in many of their students. Through that planting, I suspect that teachers genuinely approach personal immortality.

Katrina

A few weeks ago the name Katrina was just that. Few would have put any personal connection to it unless they had a friend or relative who had been given the name.

That has changed! For this generation, and for history books that follow, the word Katrina will forever mean something quite different. None of us will ever forget the vivid pictures that were beamed to us from Louisiana, Alabama, and Mississippi.

Some were quick to point fingers of political blame often giving the blame more energy than the disaster itself.

There is a biblical phrase that I often refer to in my writings, "All things work for the good." No one could ever look at this situation and say it will eventually be "good." However, the Bible phrase says that.

I'm a logical person, so I try to find logic in anything I come across. Let me try that with the verse: "In spite of bad things that happen, there can be some good to come from it."

Does that fit better? It does for me.

With this personal interpretation, let me again look at Katrina.

Hundreds of thousands of people are in need. Millions of people are available to fill part of that need. Each of us has the potential to make a difference in the life of one of those families.

Anyone who believes that it is the total responsibility of the government to provide everything to everyone is living in a fantasy world. The government is there as an umbrella for the people, but "we" are the people. We are the ones who get hurt. We are the ones who must step in to help another. We, the people, are the United States, not the government.

Individually we can make a major difference. We can donate money that can be turned into needed products. We can look in our closets and part with much of the clothes that we seldom wear.

Recently I wrote about the power of small groups. What a great time to step in with one of those groups to make a major difference.

Has your church stepped in both financially and physically? Has your church become willing to adopt a few families by bringing them to your community to help until they get on their feet? If they haven't, why not? If your church has not become a community leader in providing assistance, it may be time to find a new church.

Before long there will be another need. When the clean up begins, they will need physical labor in the affected states. When that day comes, will we become willing to give up some vacation to go and help?

I have a prayer book that I built by cutting and pasting words that I need to hear and read each day. One of the lines in a prayer says, "Use me, dear Lord, that I might know the joy of being used by you."

The word "joy" is a key word. If I want joy in my life, then I need to help another. Katrina has provided me that opportunity.

Katrina has changed our country, as did 9-11, for all time. Nevertheless, in spite of the things Katrina has caused, there can be some good to come out of it. That "good" must start with us.

Luke's Passion

Currently, my oldest son and his wife have two children. Lauren is only two months old, but Luke will soon turn 2.

Luke has already found a passion in his young life. He absolutely loves trucks and heavy equipment. He can play with his toy versions endlessly as he creates his imaginary world.

One would have thought he was in heaven when they repaired a road in his neighborhood. There it was and in real life, the full-size version of what had been captivating his world.

When I went to buy his birthday gift, I kept that in mind as I looked over the toys. Don't laugh, but I bought him a Tonka Trash Truck just like the one that picks up the trash on his street.

Luke is at the age where he can create a world he can understand and when something bigger, but similar, is introduced, he can relate to it in some fashion of growth.

Luke's dad is a professional baseball player and most times gets home around 11p.m. Because of that, Luke's mom has worked hard to adjust Luke's nap schedule so that he can often stay awake until his dad gets home.

Luke doesn't just wait, he stands in the window with only his head visible from the outside, waiting for his dad to reenter his life. My son will sometimes call me on his way home from the ballpark, and I can tell in his voice when he sees his son's head in the window.

Each day we are all introduced to a myriad of new

things. Then as time goes on we are reintroduced to it at higher and higher levels just as Luke is one day playing with his small truck and the next day he sees one that is 40 feet long.

Luke was also introduced to love by his parent's daily interaction and he can now project that daily love into greater and greater levels as he gets older.

In reverse, Luke's parents recognize their role when they see their son's dependence on them, and it is their responsibility to present themselves in a fashion that will cause Luke to grow physically, emotionally, and spiritually.

However, as he grows, his dependence on them will diminish as he starts to attach to something even more powerful than that of his parents or his Tonka Trash Truck.

I need to look around. Is there someone with their head in the window waiting on me to show God's love? Is there someone that hungers for a card or a call? Is there someone I have never met that is awaiting a loving gesture?

Define God

Have you ever tried to define God? I don't think one can accurately do so with words.

Those who have allowed God to work within their lives define it best. They do so with their action, not their words.

Passion

Did you know the ancient Greeks created an obituary after the death of each of their citizens? Where we try to list the accomplishments and memberships in our obituaries, the Greeks asked only one question: "Did he or she live with passion?"

Sure, with a little work we could all create a lengthy obituary for the paper, but would we be able to state with certainty that we "lived life with passion?"

Goal of Blaming

One of my goals is not to blame others for problems that I probably caused. The more I can do that, the more I will start to witness God working within me. Simple? If it were why will it take more than my entire life to accomplish it?

It's Not About Paperwork

Although the TV news about Katrina has diminished, the nightmare for the people affected will continue for years.

It was unfortunate that many of the politicians spent so much of their initial energy pointing fingers instead of acting. Wouldn't it be refreshing one day if they would take the same pointed fingers and use them for service toward other people?

There are two words, "why" and "what," and there is a time and a place to use each of them. For weeks we have heard from every level of government the word "why" instead of "what." "What" can be done? "What can we do to rush the needed aid?" "What" can I personally do?

No, the politicians were all stuck on the word "why." "Why wasn't this done? "Why wasn't that done?" As so often happens, the politicians had the cart in front of the horse.

Certainly, there is a time when the word "why" should be investigated and at that time the politicians can do what they do best, "talk until they are blue in the face."

The affected states can be compared to an individual struggling to breathe. Instead of providing the necessary medical treatment, the doctor asks for the proper paperwork.

Remember, life is not about "paperwork," it is about "people." It's not about "red tape," its about "service."

I learned a great lesson from the first female Admiral in the Navy. She was asked how she was able to accomplish so much in a male-dominated profession. Her response was classic, "Sir, I learned a long time ago that when something needs to be done, it is far easier to do it and then apologize versus asking for permission and then watching it never get done."

When people need help, help them and then sort out the bureaucracy later.

What Would You Die For?

What constitutes your belief system? What beliefs would you commit your life to? Ultimately, what beliefs would you die for?

Firefighters believe they have a moral obligation to protect the people they serve, no matter the personal cost.

Although we all complain about receiving a speeding ticket, police officers put their life on the line each day.

Our military may be a half a world away, but they believe that the life we so much enjoy would be compromised if they were not willing to die for it.

Mother Teresa believed so strongly that all humans were gems in the eye of God that she dedicated her entire adult life in pursuit of that belief.

We don't hear as much about Gandhi these days, but he believed so strongly that the caste system was immoral that he single handedly changed the direction of the world. He did it not by war, but by turning the other cheek.

What are we willing to commit our life to? What would we be willing to die for?

Brother Peter

In 1988 while watching a local news segment, "Spiritual Warrior," I first heard of Brother Peter and his long and arduous battle with the Chinese Communists.

So impressed was I with the interview which delved into his spiritual strength and the poignancy of his struggle, I contacted him at the Benedictine Abbey in Valyermo, California.

When I told him that I was in the music publishing business, he connected the dots making an assumption that I could help him with the book manuscript that he had been working on.

I tried to explain that **Serenity** was a music publication company and far different than companies who published books. His project was far beyond our capability. However, I did tell him I would like to read what he had written.

His manuscript talked of his 25 plus years in Chinese Communist prisons because of his Christian belief system. He described how Mao Tse Tung ordered all non-Chinese Monks out of the country. Brother Peter, being Chinese, was sent to jail instead.

He was also told that he would remain in prison until he renounced his faith.

He chose not to.

In his words he wrote of the many years of shackles, torture, and solitary confinement used in an attempt to break him.

They could not.

I soon found that Brother Peter was also a poet. In fact, a very good poet. He talked of writing poetry glorifying God, which is how he kept his sanity during those many years. However, when I say "write" it is only a figure of speech since paper and pencil were not available to the prisoners.

What he would do is create a poem in his mind and then retain it in memory. The second day he would create another poem and memorize both of them. The third day the same thing. What is astonishing is that he did this day after day, week after week, year after year filing thousands of poems away as if his mind were a file cabinet.

Much of the New Testament in the Bible was written by the Apostle Paul and he, like Brother Peter, wrote some of its most beautiful words while in prison. One can only do that when they have reached beyond their circumstances and attached to an energy greater than themselves.

I kept Br. Peter's first manuscript on a table and often thought of helping him, but my inability for rewrite, edit, and publishing always pushed the thought out of my mind. Then, in a "coincidental" conversation with my son's English teacher, I mentioned Brother Peter, his manuscript, and his desire to have it published. I asked if she would read it.

She, like me, was immediately impressed with what she read. I asked her if Brother Peter had not found a publisher, would she consider doing the rewriting and editing.

She agreed.

Having not communicated with Brother Peter for over a year, I telephoned him and expected him to tell me that he had found another company to help him.

He had not. In fact, he went on to say that during the last year he had done a complete rewrite and in hopes of convincing me to reconsider my decision, he had mailed me a revised copy of the manuscript a day earlier.

We agreed to work together and we hung up.

Within minutes the doorbell rang and a postman handed me a box which held the revised manuscript.

Not only did we complete the book, ***Dawn Breaks in the East,*** we also completed a book of his poetry, ***The Mountain Pierces the Blue Sky.***

Over the years I have spent countless hours with Brother Peter. With each visit I feel an increasing sense of personal peace. As I watch him interact with others I sense his commitment to being fully with that person. I then see him, after the conversation ends, immediately retreat into himself watching his lips move as he goes into prayer.

Throughout our lives each of us cross paths with countless people. Some of these have a great influence upon us. But there are just a few, very few, that literally change the course of our lives. For me, Brother Peter is one of those people.

The best way to know Br. Peter is through his writing. Let me share one of his poems and as you read his words and experience his feelings, realize how his life experiences have brought him to a level of awareness that far exceeds his body:

Ten summers in the prison of Peng'an
Were hot as the burning sun,
But five months in a solitary cell
Were sweet as honeyed wine.
Added penalty,
Threats and criticism
Did not wear down my will;
Binding ropes,
Beatings and insults
Harmed only my body.

We are the Support

Yesterday morning I spoke with a woman who had called with questions about our music. Within moments I knew that her questions were really about deeper issues, and she had come to us hoping the music would solve those issues.

As we talked I explained to her that our music would not provide the answers she was looking for. Rather, the music would provide an atmosphere of support for her as she searched for the answers.

I suggested that many things presented to us in life do not give us answers, but actually provide supportive opportunities to deal with our hurt.

For example, a 12-Step program is not the final answer for the drinker. It is a support system to help one to stay away from the addictive alcohol.

Churches do not give us answers. They provide a path toward the answers, but it is up to us to decide if we will follow that path.

The lady who called explained that she has really struggled since her brother's unexpected death and the emptiness that followed. I offered her various programs to help her deal with the emptiness explaining that none of them would remove the hurt; they would only help her to deal with the hurt. Loss is loss and there is nothing soft or simple about it.

We talked more than 45 minutes, and at the end of the conversation she said that she felt so much better. She thanked me for doing that. I quickly explained that I had not done anything other than offer her support as she talked about her hurt.

I gave her no answers. I gave her support so she could gain the strength to work toward finding her answers.

We all carry "hurt and pain" and I often go to my support system. My friends and my 12-Step group do not give me answers, but they do offer an opportunity for me to hand them my hurt, through words, so I can catch my breath. Then, with great wisdom they hand back my problems and I, now a bit stronger, am better able to deal with the issue.

As I write this, we are approaching the Christmas season. It is also the season when pain, loss, and loneliness are manifested. Be alert to that with your friends.

Remember that we cannot give our friends the answers, but we can give them a gift that far exceeds anyone's expectation. The gift of friendship and a listening ear.

Everything Emanates

My belief is that everything emanates from God, the source of all energy. When we become willing to help another, we are the recipients of God's energy in support of that willingness.

I often say that love, when given, continues for all time, never ending. I suspect that love is nothing less than the highest form of energy on earth.

How is it that this energy, or love, continues? Those of us who have a science background were taught about the Laws of Thermodynamics. It states that energy cannot be created or destroyed, it can only be converted.

For example, I go to the gas station and buy a gallon of gas. This gallon of gas has a certain amount of "potential energy." We can see it instantly dissipated by tossing a lit match into the container. We can also take the gallon of gas, inject it into the carburetor of our car and by adding a spark from the spark plug, its "potential energy" is converted through the engine, transmission, drive shaft, and eventually providing energy to turn the wheels of the vehicle.

The energy in the gasoline was not destroyed, it was converted.

Maybe this is the way we are with God's love, or should I say God's loving energy. Like the gallon of gas, the loving energy is always available, free for the asking and never running out. All we have to do it choose to tap into it. Then, like the Law of Thermodynamics states, it can be converted and used to help another person. That person, now touched by the healing energy, has the renewed strength to go to another to offer help.

That's what life is all about. It is the recognition of the Spiritual Laws of Thermodynamics: God's love cannot be created or destroyed. It is always there. It is given freely, traveling through all time, healing all it touches.

Who is That Looking Over Your Shoulder?

"What would you do if no one was looking?"

I have read that question a hundred times in the last couple of years. Each time I do, I stop and reflect on the words and its application to my life.

You would have laughed at me a couple weeks ago when I crawled around on the ground reaching under my car to retrieve a piece of trash that had blown out of my car door.

With no one around I could have easily ignored it. However, I was not alone. With me was the most critical person I know, my "higher self." Like it or not, no matter where I go or what I do, I have this constant companion with me. Sure, I can ignore "my higher self," but by doing so, I would not be true to myself.

Have you ever walked along a road and looked into the ditch? What you see is an endless amount of trash that was tossed by individuals who felt no one was looking.

This is just a small example of what is infecting a large part of our society today. What is the illness? It is the disease of ignoring our "higher self." When we do, we ignore our connection with God thus allowing all that is less than good to infect us.

Our days are made up of moments in which we must make personal decisions. With that in mind, my question to myself is this: Would my decision change if I knew someone was looking over my shoulder? Someone is. It is me.

Do You Pray?

Do you pray? If so, why do you pray? Is it to influence this power we call God?

I have always struggled with this question. Let me suggest a different thought: Maybe prayer is not something we do to influence God, but rather something we do to better prepare ourselves to receive the good that God is always doing.

Outside Myself

We all have the desire to look outward to find happiness. I would find it if only I would lose some weight or have nicer clothes. I would be happy if I had a bigger house or if I had "body fix-it" surgery. If. If. If.

I may be wrong, but from personal experience I've concluded that if I can't find peace of mind within myself, I sure as hell won't find it outside of myself!

Wednesdays With Bill

The church I attend is committed to helping others. They don't just talk about it, they do it!

The list of projects would fill several pages, stretching from the orphanages of Cambodia to the homeless on Southern California's local streets.

Therefore, when our minister talked of a member family needing help, we all listened.

He described a family that many of the church members already knew. In the family was a gentleman in the late stages of Lou Gehrig's disease.

My knowledge of the disease was somewhat limited to its being named for a famous New York Yankees ballplayer who had been afflicted. I also knew that Morrie, in the book, ***Tuesdays With Morrie,*** was afflicted with the same disease. Later I read that in medical talk it is actually Amyotrophic Lateral Sclerosis (ALS). It is a progressive neurodegenerative disease that affects nerve cells in the brain and the spinal cord.

It is also terminal.

Having no idea what this family might need, I decided I would at least look into it.

Our church has a central courtyard where hundreds of people congregate before and after each church service. It is also where church groups exhibit their information, making it available to all members. If one walks through the courtyard and does not feel needed, they certainly have a problem.

In this case, I could not find anything that would give me additional information about the family in need.

After criss-crossing the courtyard a few more times, I gave up and started towards the exit door leaving the courtyard. As I approached it, a young lady and baby approached the door also. Since the child was about the same age as one of my grandchildren, I asked a question or two about the child as I reached to open the door.

Without thinking, I asked her if she had been in the last service and if she had any idea where the information might be for the family in need. With more than a thousand people in church and courtyard to choose from, I chose her. She responded, "I have no idea if there is an information booth, but the person with Lou Gehrig's disease is my dad."

She told me that her dad's name is Bill, in his mid-50's, with symptoms starting to appear seven years earlier. We chatted a bit longer, and at the end of the conversation I gave her my telephone number.

The following day I received a call from Sue, the young woman's mother and Bill's wife. After talking about Bill, I asked her how I could be most helpful to their needs.

She was specific. She needed a caregiver on Wednesday mornings so she could continue working, providing the family an income and health insurance.

She invited me to their home to get a better idea of what I might be walking into. This also gave her an opportunity to see how I would interact with Bill.

The disease had progressed leaving Bill with the ability to track me with his eyes and the ability to move the right side of his lip just slightly.

A ventilator did his breathing and a stomach tube provided a path for his liquid food.

To the casual observer, one would see a man that is left with an inability to do anything.

Nothing could be farther from the truth.

My first meeting with Bill was last year. Since then, he and I have spent our Wednesday mornings together. We talk, and sometimes argue, mostly about baseball. No, he doesn't argue with words, it is just the way he moves the side of his lip when he doesn't agree with me.

To keep track of insulin shots, Bill's stomach is dotted by a felt tip pen, as well as autographs from his young grandchildren.

With a couple of his grandchildren attending an elementary school across the street, family members visit with Bill nearly every morning. Each talk to him, but the very young crawl up on the bed as if they are on a jungle gym at the local park. After they plant a kiss on his forehead, the side of his mouth moves slightly as it forms a million-dollar smile.

I watch his wife interact with him as I witness a deep love that few of us will ever experience. I also see the pain and longing in his eyes as he watches Sue leave for work.

Bible study groups and friends continue to surround the family. On Sunday, while most of us are finding rationalizations to stay in bed, Bill and Sue attend church.

Anyone who knows the prognosis of Lou Gehrig's disease, knows that Bill is living on borrowed time. He may not be able to move his body, but nothing has prevented his heart from continuing to give love to all who meet him.

If you need to reach me, check your calendar. If it is a Wednesday morning, I will not be in the office because I am blessed to spend my "Wednesdays with Bill."

Family on Veterans Day

Today is Veterans Day. It is always a tough day for me. Being in the military (Vietnam era), I cannot escape the memories of a time passed.

Although many businesses prosper during a time of war, no rational person wants to see any of our citizens in harm's way. We want peace, but we also need a strong military. I often remind people who argue that we need to dismantle the military that they need to imagine what would happen to their town if there were no police department. The military is to the free world as the police are to our local communities.

In the same moment, I could vigorously argue both sides as to being in Iraq or not. However, that is not the purpose of this reflection. Each of us must personally deal with that issue.

When I returned from my overseas tour, I was booed, pelted with rotten food when I left the base, and called most of the four-letter words. When my wife joined me in Japan while on leave, we were treated as criminals often shoved out of trains, ignored by taxis, denied service in restaurants, and also called various names in Japanese. Having no choice, we walked mile after mile with my wife obviously pregnant.

Fortunately today our troops are recognized for their sacrifices, not the political views of the government.

There is a country western singer, John Conlee, who sings a song called, "They Also Served." It is about the families and friends of those serving.

No one would argue that I was at a high level of

risk when flying on and off an aircraft carrier at night. But when I was back on the deck, my food was prepared, my room was cleaned, my clothes were washed, and my day was planned for me. All I had to do was get into a plane, do what I was trained to do, and complete my mission.

During that same time frame, my wife was about to have a baby, and did so while I was gone. Because of my below-average military income, she continued to work, saddled with overwhelming bills, keeping the house up, and the strain of wondering if her husband would return alive.

She was not alone. Every veteran's family has to sacrifice in much the same way. For most, it is done in silence.

Conlee, in his song "They Also Served," brings that silence to light. In his rusty country voice he will bring tears to the eyes of all who hear it.

Tonight when you are around your family or sitting back thinking peaceful thoughts about them, give gratitude to the veteran's and to their families who also, as the song says, are tucking their kids in bed trying to explain why their mommy or daddy is not there.

One of My Heroes

One of my heroes died recently. She was not a person who gained fame for great invention or great financial success.

Her fame came from a spontaneous decision by "standing up," or in this case, "not standing up" against those oppressing others.

Rosa Parks was a small frail woman who, like so many others, went to work each day on public transportation.

Whether her decision was spontaneous or the outcome of years of frustration, it took great courage to stand up against someone who thought their race was superior to her black heritage.

Although she could have easily been hung for such a stance, her single decision changed the course of American history. She did not do it with guns and violence, but with a gracious voice by just saying "no" to the person who demanded she give up her seat and move to the back of the bus.

Although her decision was based on race, much of what she stood for can be projected into other areas of non-racial applications today.

We are in a time when large businesses continue to gobble up smaller businesses at an alarming rate. What used to be a check-and-balance system of fairness in competition has all but been dismantled. In so doing, employees are discarded and the department of "customer service" should be renamed "customer disservice." It has all been done in the name of money, power, and stockholder demands.

When Rosa Parks stood up to her oppressors, she had no idea that anyone would join her in support. In fact, that was the last thing on her mind as she was only trying to defend her own humanness in that particular moment.

Maybe if the U.S. had a few more Rosa Parks walking among us, we could again have a say in shaping our government, businesses, and organizations that have forgotten that it is about "people," not money and power.

Rosa, thanks for listening to the "spirit of right and wrong" that resides in each of us.

Christmas Shopping

Are you finished with your Christmas shopping?

Have all the people on your Christmas list been accounted for?

If you are like me your list includes family, close friends, and people who have been special in your life this past year.

For most of us, there is another list. Unpublished. On it are people who have offended us, caused us pain, or haven't lived up to our "invented" expectations of them. They are the people we do not necessarily like.

Take a few moments and create a list of those people. Now, how would you like to give yourself a gift that is greater than any gift that can be bought in a store? Take a second look at your "resentment" list that is stealing so much of your peace of mind.

Is there something we can do with the list?

One of the steps in the 12-Step program says to make a list of all persons who we have harmed, and become willing to make amends to them all.

The next step asks us to "Make direct amends to such people wherever possible, except when to do so would injure them or others."

In most problems there are two sides. Our egos have a way of looking at a problem and assigning total blame to another person. This Christmas take ego out of the loop when you look at your "resentment" list.

Where possible, we should contact these people. Discard the ego's "blame" card and substitute "amends" in its place.

When we have done that, then we truly have completed everything on our Christmas list.

It is then that we receive God's greatest gift, "spiritual healing."

Christmas Spirit

It's that time of the year for everyone to talk about "Christmas Spirit." In all honesty, what do those words mean?

If I did a survey of 100 people, I would probably receive a hundred different definitions.

After I heard myself tell a customer that there seemed to be a decline in "Christmas Spirit" in recent years, I wondered what I had really said.

What is "Christmas Spirit"? Once I read that a conscious decision to offer someone something and expect absolutely nothing in return is one of the kindest things one can do.

I think those words would describe it.

If so, then "Christmas Spirit" is really another way of saying unconditional love for another during the holidays.

Here is a small gesture I witnessed a couple years ago that still affects me when I think of it.

It was close to Christmas and the parking lots at the mall were packed. I had already parked my car and was walking across the lot when I saw two cars converging on a single spot that was starting to open up. Both arrived at the emptying spot at nearly the same moment.

Now what, I thought as I stopped to watch.

It took less than a few seconds for one of the two cars to back up allowing the other car into the spot.

Immediately, an elderly gentleman who had just parked his car got out and immediately walked over to the person who had allowed him into the spot.

I could hear him say "Thank you."

From the other car I could hear a woman say, "You're welcome, Merry Christmas."

I would suspect both of them were feeling the "Christmas Spirit" during their chance meeting.

It Is What It Is

"It is what it is."

I use this statement often. I understand that I may not be able to control "it," but I do control how I view "is."

Who are You?

Who are we? Are we who others tell us to be? Are we what our ego has demanded? On the other hand, are we a reflection of God?

In each moment, we have a choice to make.

Giving and Loving

Something to think about. If you want others to be happy, be giving and loving. If you want to be happy, be giving and loving.

Music as an Excuse

I've been working with the creation of music since 1985. I know how important music has been in the lives of many people struggling to find peace of mind. However, when I take a step back, I realize that our creating the music has a more important purpose. It is spirit's method of providing an excuse for two of us to come together and help each other on our path, following in line with "where two or three are gathered…"

Yesterday I received a telephone call from an elderly gentleman asking that I remove his wife's name from our mailing list. Ironically, he received our new flyer on what would have been their 52nd wedding anniversary. With her death a couple months earlier, he had moved from the stage of numbness and was now fully entrenched in raw pain.

After assuring him we would abide by his request, I asked him to tell me more about his wife.

After he told me how much it hurt to see her name on an envelope, I made a suggestion. When an envelope arrives with her name, he should take the letter, hold it in both hands, and look at her name. While doing so give thanks to God for having put her in his life.

I went on to suggest that if he did this with each letter, he would each time grieve for her a bit more. And each time he grieved her loss, he would empty out a bit more of his aching heart allowing a bit more of God's love in.

His next question surprised me and told me that he did not have a support system, "What do you mean by grieving?"

I suggested that in simple terms it was nothing more than putting a picture of his wife into his mind and allowing the emotions of his body to do whatever they wanted. If he felt like crying, cry. If he felt like throwing a dish across the kitchen, do it. If he felt like telling God off, have at it. Grieving is looking right into the eyes of all the pain and facing it.

He then asked, "You mean if I cry every time I see her name, that is okay?"

I told him it was not only okay, it was normal! I also told him that as time went on there would be a day when he would not cry when he saw her name. In fact, there would be a day when a smile would come to his face.

I also explained that the healing that would take place over time was not an indication of his forgetting her. Rather, healing would better be described as gaining the strength to tolerate the pain of her loss.

By the end of the conversation, I could sense a bit of relief in his voice. He seemed to understand that everything he was feeling was normal and the pain was a direct reflection of the deep love he had had for his wife.

I reminded him that "grieving pain is the unfortunate cost of a lifetime of committed love." I don't think that you can have one without the other.

Politically Correct

Are you confused about using the words "Merry Christmas?" How about "Happy Holidays?" The question that has been asked repeatedly this year is whether we are "politically correct." Are you? I hope not. I hope I am not either.

Personally, it would not bother me if I never heard the term, "politically correct" again.

Over the decades our moral fiber, which is born in the "heart," has been eroded while our self-centered thinking, invented in our "heads," has taken more and more control.

In other words, caring and compassion come from the "heart" while manipulation and self-centered thinking come from the "head."

Anyone who has read stories about our Founding Fathers would understand that our country was founded on what is right in the heart, not the "politically correct" head.

Today, for example, look at Congress. Most are no longer searching for "what is right," as they work non-stop to garner power. "Power" is of the head while "what is right" is born in the heart.

This same attitude is now being applied to the term "Christmas." When I think of Christmas, the words "caring and compassionate" come to mind. When I think of Hanukkah, I think of the same words. However, our "politically correct" society is doing their best to drive us away from "heart" and into the "head."

When I wish someone "Merry Christmas" or "Happy Hanukkah" I am really saying, "I give you, from the deepest part of my heart, my best."

Growing up in the farm country of the Midwest, I learned that it is traditional to say "hi" to people when you meet them on the street, even if you don't know them.

Some say that if I wish you "Merry Christmas" and you are Jewish, I would be embarrassing you and putting you in an awkward position. Others say that if my Jewish friends wish me a Happy Hanukkah, it will embarrass me. Not true. If I am Christian and offer you a "Merry Christmas," I am offering you my very best. If you respond in kind, I know you are offering me the same.

So, my heart felt words of "Merry Christmas" or a response of "Happy Hanukkah" to my Jewish friends means the same—I acknowledge you as a child of God.

Power Greater Than Self

Are troubles causing fear in your life? From experience, I think fear is the method that problems make themselves known in our lives.

Fears have the potential to take control of our lives, if we allow them. I used to think that facing the fears was the only thing necessary to make them better. It made sense. However, for whatever reason, the problems would look as if they were disappearing and then reoccur in some other form.

Over time I've come to believe that my method of problem solution was flawed. It appears that if I create a problem at a certain level of energy, trying to solve it at that same level of energy would not work. As someone said in a 12-Step meeting, "If your way did not prevent the problem, then why do you think your way will now solve the problem?"

I thought long and hard about what he said and had a one-on-one discussion with myself. "God, what did he mean? If I caused the problem then he says I cannot solve the problem. If I can't, then who will?"

Lots of years and many personal stupid mistakes have taught me the limitations of my abilities. Seldom have I been able to individually solve the problems I have caused.

Here's a story about a young man attending his first 12-Step meeting. Because of a drunken driving arrest, the court had ordered him to attend these meetings against his will. He was unhappy and determined to take control.

He ranted and raved for several minutes as he condemned the court, the police officer who arrested him, the judge, the 12-Step program, and pretty much the world in general.

Finally an old-time member spoke. "Son, I know what you're saying. I used to feel the same way, but let's review your life for a moment. You seem to be pretty smart. You have a lifetime of experience and knowledge. Let's put all of that together and see where it got you." He paused. "It got you all the way to this meeting tonight. That's what your abilities alone have given you. Let me offer to you the exact words that were given to me many years ago. Number one: Shut up. Number two: Start listening. Number three: Keep bringing your butt to meetings and maybe one day your brain will follow."

What this old-timer was also emphasizing was that we cannot solve our own problems at the same level we created them. To solve them we need to tap into a power greater than ourselves to bring the needed "solutional" energy in.

In a 12-Step program, the group is a power that is greater than the individual. Over time the individual finds that there is even a greater power than the group. Most of us call that power, God.

Many churches are pushing to form small groups within the larger church to offer individuals a place to bring their problems on a regular basis. When they do, the group, along with the power of prayer, brings a higher collective energy to the problem.

So, how do we solve problems? I don't think we

can. My experience continues to show me that long-term solutions to my problems come when I take the problem to a power greater than I. This power is where overwhelming energy, originating with God, can dissipate the problem for all time.

Fear Reduces

I was told that there are 365 references in the Bible that imply that fear reduces our energy.

Stuff

A thought for this Christmas season: It's not about stuff. Sure, stuff can bring you pleasure, but pleasure is not happiness. Pleasure ultimately disappears, happiness is infinite.

Is God in Heaven?

I have often prayed for changes to take place. I've struggled with this "God in heaven" that we pray to. Maybe, just maybe, the words saying that the "kingdom of heaven is within you" are accurate. If so, then maybe our prayers should be directed inward, not to some foreign and distant place in the sky.

It's Christmas Day

It's Christmas Day! If you're looking for a gift, maybe there is one for you under the tree.

If you're looking for the greatest gift, look into the eyes of your family and friends.

Maybe the person attached to those eyes is not available. Maybe God has called them home. Maybe those eyes live in another part of the country. Maybe those eyes are in a foreign country protecting our freedom. If so, then look into the eyes of a blessed memory and bring that memory into focus.

As you stare into their eyes or into the eyes from the memory past, let the feelings of love surround you. As you do, let the feelings of love engulf you. As you do, let the feelings of love warm every cell of your being.

Then, as you feel that love on this Christmas day, remember the *first* Christmas, the Christmas that taught us that the greatest gift of all is love.

C.S. Lewis

The world is discovering C.S. Lewis.

A couple of years ago I recommended his book on grief to a friend. At that time, a bookstore may have had a couple of his many books but no more than that.

Since then, I have watched, with great fascination as interest in his writing has substantially grown. Granted, much of the current interest is caused by the movie, "The Chronicles of Narnia."

I became familiar with his works when my sons were young and their mother would read the Chronicles to them. I believe those books had a major impact on their spiritual growth.

Norman Stone has released a documentary on C.S. Lewis. He says that the reason the Chronicle books have been so successful is that they meet the reader at their level. For some, they will provide only entertainment. Others will be taken beyond the entertainment and see that the books are introducing something with greater meaning.

Stone believes that the entire meaning of Christianity is imbedded in the books.

Country singer Naomi Judd said her actor daughter, Ashley, read the Chronicles at age 8 and, according to Naomi, fashioned much of her spiritual life around the Chronicles.

I think I have been drawn to Lewis because he was not a holy man. Like me, he spent a great part of his life struggling with the word "religion."

Do yourself a favor. Introduce you and your family, if you haven't already, to the life and writings of C.S. Lewis.

Gratitude

I often bring up the subject of gratitude. It is being thankful for what has been presented to us. No, I won't argue with anyone who says that life hands out many problems that make it hard to be grateful.

If one is not thinking of gratitude, it is hard to recognize the good that does happen.

On the lighter side, I recently heard a person say, "I read the paper in bed everyday. I start with the obituaries. If I don't find my name listed, I give gratitude and then get up and get on with my day."

I guess "being given another day" should be the first line on our gratitude list each day. Those who have lost someone close to them know exactly what I mean.

"Why me?"

"Why me" is often the first question from my mouth after something unwanted or painful happens in my life.

If so, when joy happens in my life why is not my first question, "Why me?"

Peacebringers

Many have the ability to step in after a problem has been created and become peacemakers. Often relationships are made up of partners who spend lots of time doing just that.

Here is a thought from one of America's great poets, Maya Angelou: Maybe more important than being a peacemaker is becoming a peacebringer.

After I heard that statement, I reflected on it and wrote down a couple of thoughts that could become an endless list:

- When you get something, be a giver of something.
- When you learn something, become a teacher of what you have learned.
- When you are hurt, become a forgiver.
- When you struggle, allow others to help.

Sure, we are all human and we often cause problems for others. When we do, become a peacemaker. Then work even harder at becoming a peacebringer.

Half Measures?

This morning I received a telephone call from a regular customer who purchases CDs to give to each of the women she counsels—all of whom have breast cancer.

Recently a dear friend of mine started chemotherapy for breast cancer.

After lunch, I called the woman who has been cutting my hair for probably 25 years. She is in the middle of her second bout with breast cancer.

I don't think a day goes by that I don't receive a call from a breast-cancer patient or a friend who is hoping to find supportive music or guided imagery.

We are a country of great diversity. Maybe too diverse at times. By trying to do a little bit of something for everyone, we ultimately accomplish little or nothing.

In the 12-Step program they say that "Half measures avail us nothing." Rephrased, to be fully successful, one must be fully committed to what one is doing.

That applies to many of our government programs as well. Nearly all of them are "half-measures" programs and never seem to solve the problem they were intended to fix.

Breast cancer is one of those areas. We have businesses and government agencies that are involved in cancer research. However, we as a country have no concerted commitment.

Decades ago we had a dedicated commitment to put a man on the moon. It was a total commitment and nothing was going to get in its way. Nothing did.

One could argue that the government might not

have enough money to "commit" to solving breast cancer as we once "committed" to getting to the moon. I disagree. For example, as long as we have millions of dollars to build an Alaskan bridge that goes from "nowhere" to "nowhere" and unwanted by the Alaskans, we have available money. If given a few minutes I could list hundreds, if not thousands, of programs that have little or no value other than power accumulation.

It's hard not to complain when elected officials, holding the potential for many positive solutions, accomplish so little.

Breast cancer, like many problems, can be solved—but can only be done so with a concerted and committed effort. One cannot forget the universal law that states, "half measures avail us nothing."

Lesson from the Miners

Earlier this week we, as a country, were transported to the mines of West Virginia.

Without warning, an explosion occurred and instantly thirteen men became isolated from the rest of the world.

All of us clung to hope as every technical advance was used to obtain additional information hoping for their eventual recovery.

I happened to be awake and watched the announcement that they were all "alive." I was still awake when the announcement was made that they were "not alive."

I could not imagine what it would have been like for the families to experience the "ups" and then "downs."

I felt the anger of the friends and relatives, and I understood their resentment at the company that may have not been as responsive to safety as they should have been.

All of this is sad and most unfortunate and will be investigated.

Then out of the darkness came a revelation that these men were more than victims; they were teachers of God.

As the men awaited, knowing they were about to die, they made a decision to detach from the fear of death and chose to connect to love instead. Instead of writing about death, they became poets as they jotted down their deepest feelings for their loves ones. Instead of wasting time writing about their anger of the situation presented to them, they wrote about the peacefulness of the moment telling all of us that their death was not causing physical pain.

There were telling us that the most important moment was the "present moment" and they chose to use that moment to discuss love instead of anything else.

We all have the potential to live in that "moment" and we all have potential to look beyond our problems to see the only thing that really matters.

It's All About Miracles

We at **Serenity** receive letters, calls, and emails from appreciative listeners nearly every day. Even after all these years I am still humbled by every one.

Last night I received a short email from a person by the name of Teri. She went on to say that she was "so happy to have again found us after all these years" and she wanted to obtain another copy of ***Miracles***, the first music we did over 20 years ago.

I sent a short reply to her and suggested she call me at her convenience. The next morning we connected by telephone and she proceeded to tell me of her connection to the album ***Miracles*** and how important it had been to her.

She told me she was invited to a baby shower and she wanted to provide the baby with a bit of music. She went on to say that she had purchased a lullaby CD at a store and hoped it would have the same effect on the new baby as our ***Miracles*** album had on her now grown son.

She then read to me a letter she had written to the new mother:

"I had a tape that I used to play for Jonathan every night from soon after he was born until he left elementary school. His father and I took it on trips with us, when visiting friends and relatives—everywhere. It was music that signaled to him it was time to rest, have some peace, and be alone to enjoy the music. It helped him sleep and was comforting to him every night. To this day, his 17th year, he remembers the tune and rhythm of the tape. That tape was called ***Miracles*** and

I'm sure it doesn't exist anymore. I hope this CD will bring you and your baby the same peace and comfort it brought to us."

After she finished writing this beautiful note, it occurred to her that with the Internet she could at least take a moment to make sure her statement that "I'm sure it doesn't exist anymore" was accurate.

I listened as she described her delight when her "search words" took her to **Serenity** and reintroduced her to a bit of her past.

After ordering, she gave me her address in Huntington Beach, California. I told her my son and his wife also lived in the same town, and we concluded that they only lived a couple blocks apart.

As we talked, I told her that I had been in her area just a few weeks earlier and met my son and his wife at this great restaurant.

When she asked the name, I stuttered as I tried to remember. Finally I told her it was "Stone..., Stone…, Stone something."

"Stone Fire?" she asked.

"Yes, that's it! It was some of the best food I've ever eaten. Their Tri-Tip BBQ was incredible. If I could move it next door to me I would!"

As I tried to complete my sentence I could tell that Teri was trying her best to interrupt me.

"Jim, Jim. That baby shower that I've been invited to?"

"Yes."

"The person I want to give the ***Miracles*** CD to?"

"Yes."

"Well you aren't going to believe this. She runs the Stone Fire Grill!"

We both laughed as we talked about the big world that we live in that isn't so big.

Is there a moral to the story? I don't know. I do know that when Rob Whitesides-Woo, the composer of the ***Miracles*** album, and I finished it in 1985, (yes, 1985) we knew it was special.

When asked through the years, Rob always said that he didn't write the music. He just put the pen to paper and the fingers to the musical instruments and God took over from there.

We sometimes say that certain music is "timeless." Maybe "timeless" is another way of saying, "Divinely inspired."

If an album is "inspired" then it will continue to touch one's heart as it travels from generation to generation.

Teri, her husband, and Jonathan were touched and they felt the desire to carry the ***Miracles*** album forward to allow it to touch another generation.

Why did my son choose the restaurant? I'd like to think there is another inspired reason for that, but I would not know what that might be.

I do know that I will again go the **Stone Fire Grill** and when I do, I hope to meet the mother of the "soon to be born baby."

Maybe more will be revealed at that time. Then again, if not, I know that I'll have some of the best food one could ever taste. You know, the kind that food critics sometimes call "divine."

Being a Counselor

Many years ago I was a Family Counselor. Armed with all of this education I set out to impart my wisdom upon the families and individuals put in my path. "Telling them what they had to do to make their lives better" was my methodology.

After some time, I realized that my method was not working and I had to take a step back and reevaluate.

Months earlier, one of my professors, a therapist, told our counseling class that, "Some of the best counseling one can ever do is to keep one's mouth shut and just listen."

I took his advice and saw immediate results. In fact, it was common to be told by the client after a session how helpful the hour had been. Often I may have said nothing more than a sentence or two.

I suspect that each of us has a unique path buried within and awaiting to guide us to true peace of mind. If I, the counselor, start to impart my thoughts onto you, I may be sending you down a road that was not spiritually designed for you.

On the other hand, if I'm willing to listen to what you express, your words will tell both you and me where you are and what road your spirit asks you to follow.

The same applies to each of us as friends. We all know that if we offer a "listening ear" we can be helpful. I don't think I have ever heard that if we offer a "talking mouth" it would be of much value.

Again from personal experience, if I'm unwilling

to listen to you then I am probably as unwilling to listen to the intuitive words of God.

If I thrive on telling you what to do, I probably tell God how to run things as well.

I receive telephone calls each day from people who are struggling with personal issues and are hopeful that our music and guided imagery might help.

Little do they know how helpful "they" are to me. I have a prayer that is taped to my computer monitor: "God, please bring people to me today who I may be able to help. God, please bring people to me today who can help me. Amen."

That is the key to being a good counselor or a good friend. When two people come together, subconsciously both parties are givers. In addition, both parties are receivers.

Giving and receiving are equally the same.

I have found that those who come to **Serenity** with the greatest pain are always the ones who become my greatest teachers. However, the teaching would never take place if, during the telephone call, I did not have a willingness to listen.

The greatest gift we can ever "give a friend" is a willingness to listen.

The greatest gift we can ever "give ourselves" is a willingness to listen.

Then the sign, quoting the Psalms that hangs above my desk, takes on greater meaning, "Be still and know that I am God."

Stuck in My Comfort Zone

Here I am again sitting in my comfort zone. Maybe "comfort" is the wrong word since it implies that it is comfortable to be there. Maybe I should call it an "existence" zone.

It is a zone in which I am not growing. I am just existing. I'm not productive. I'm not helping others. I'm alive, but not much more than that. Nothing!

Since I've done this "comfort or existence" zone so often, I feel that I am an expert. In addition, to survive at this level of "nothingness" one needs only one piece of equipment, a TV.

Yes, a TV can turn me into a vegetable faster than anything known to man. TV has an invisible shield which encompasses the viewer, keeping anything of value from ever reaching me.

It blocks the discovery of one's purpose in life by anesthetizing the brain.

Oh, I know there are times that the TV sends me something positive. However, this happens so seldom that I normally miss it.

Over time, even the heartiest TV viewers start to feel a yearning from within; a gut feeling that there may be something more to life than "Gilligan's Island."

I suspect the yearning is a spiritual call, with boundless energy, that has been patiently waiting, like a wall plug, for me to tap into.

Not Proud Of

My background has been dotted with many actions that I am far from being proud.

During a recent 12-Step meeting, I listened to a young man literally beat himself up for every past mistake he had made.

Although he had less than two months in the 12-Step program, his words spoke directly to me.

As he continued, I realized that I have come a long way, but I also realized that I am a long way from the destination. You've heard the statement about "seeing the light at the end of the tunnel?" There are days that my tunnel doesn't have much light!

Finally, a member with years of sobriety spoke up. "Son, I learned a long time ago that I can't change the stupid things I've done, but I can do a lot to change the stupid guy who had done all of those stupid things."

He was right. We can do nothing in going backward to change what we've done. In fact, if we could change our past most of us would spend the majority of our day in reverse.

Will we make mistakes? Absolutely! When we do, we need to accept responsibility for our actions, make amends with those we have hurt, and then make sure the spiritual car is no longer in "reverse," but has been put into "drive" and headed forward.

Who Do You Wish You Had Been?

Many years ago I was asked whom I wanted to be when I grew up.

Since I was already grown, I took the question to mean, "whom I wanted to be if I could be someone else."

I couldn't answer the question, but I did think about it as I let the names of many famous people float through my mind. Whom would I want to be if I could? I did not know. Maybe astronaut Neil Armstrong, or one of the writers John Grisham or Nicholas Sparks, or humanitarian Albert Schweitzer.

A few years ago, I was reading a book about the life of Nobel Prize winner, George Bernard Shaw. Late in life he was asked if there was anyone he wished he could have been. Instantly I thought of the question presented to me decades earlier.

He responded, "Yes." He said he wished he had been George Bernard Shaw, the George Bernard Shaw that he could have become and never became.

It was over 20 years between the time I was asked the original question and my reading about Shaw. Occasionally something would trigger that question, but I never, not even once, thought about the "me" becoming "me," the "real me."

As is often the case, we look outside of ourselves for greatness, but true greatness comes from our journey inward to become the full expression of what God intended us to be.

As I've gotten older I've come to believe that true

genius does not come from the diplomas on the wall, but rather from diplomas generated by life experiences worn on our heart.

Ever hear of Rich Donato? I doubt it. I had not either until I saw a story about him on the **Hallmark Channel**.

Rich's occupation was janitor at a California high school. As the teachers taught from the books, he made himself available to listen to the students and teach from his heart. He encouraged them. He guided them. He disciplined them. He cried with them. He laughed with them. He motivated them.

Then, by chance, it was discovered that he had never graduated from high school, a new requirement for employment in the school district. His dyslexia and Attention Deficit Disorder had prevented him from being able to complete high school.

Given 30 days to either graduate or obtain a GED (an equivalency diploma), he immediately took the exam and failed miserably.

When word spread through the school, the students and teachers rallied around him going to extremes to help him remember the important facts expected on the test.

Down to the last day, he needed an 81% to pass the exam.

He fell a point short and in the eyes of the administration, he failed. In spite of his tremendous influence on the kids and his undying commitment to their success, he was fired.

Later it was discovered that the district had made a

mistake in requiring Rich to obtain a diploma because of the "grandfather clause" that accompanied the new rule.

He accepted reinstatement with a guarantee that nothing like this would ever happen again. However, if he were going to talk about motivation to the kids, he would have to be motivated in his own heart. He did just that and opted for the path of most resistance and continued working until he finally passed his GED.

Overload

In the early 1970's I was an RF-4 Phantom jet pilot in the military. Because of my reconnaissance specialty, I often had to fly at night off an aircraft carrier.

If "carrier" and "night" weren't enough, we also had to do many of our missions at high speed and low altitude.

With all of these risk variables, the most valuable lesson any pilot can ever learn is to evaluate every "current situation," as it happens, and then apply what one just learned to the next "current situation."

One night we were returning to the carrier after completing a mission. The weather was calm, but foggy. Very foggy!

As my "backseater" (the RF-4 aircraft has a person in the back seat who does all the navigating and provides advice to the pilot who is in the front seat) and I prepared to descend into the fog, he told me that he would give me incremental updates using the two words, "fog" or "clear." This would allow me to keep my eyes glued to the instrument panel helping to keep the wings level and our rate of descent under control.

In my ear was another input from a radar controller, buried in the belly of the aircraft carrier, giving me further advice about left/right or up/down as compared to the perfect glide slope.

If that wasn't enough to think about, the tiny runway attached to the carrier was propelled through the ocean at over 20-mph.

Pitch dark, we started down the glide slope.

From the controller came, "Left 2," meaning go

left 2 degrees.

From the backseat, "Fog."

From the controller, "Slightly below glide slope."

"Fog."

"Right 3."

"Fog."

"Slightly above glide slope."

"Going further above glide slope."

"Fog."

Everything I did to the aircraft was based on the information I had just received. "Current situation" to update the previous "current situation."

At approximately one mile from landing things immediately change. The pilot is to convert from the instruments to the ship's mirror system that uses reflective light to update the pilot during final seconds before landing. If above the optimum glide slope, the reflective light looks high. If below the optimum glide slope, the reflective light looks low.

In addition, we are handed over from the radar controller, who has been updating us as we descended, to the deck-based controller called a Landing Signal Officer (LSO). This person, also a pilot, has years of training and can sense minor changes in the attitude of the physical aircraft even before the pilot can sense it and then offer immediate advice. Without question, the aircrew learns to put their lives in the hands of the LSO.

"3/4 mile, call the ball." These are the first words from the LSO who is asking me if I can see the reflective mirror system and to acknowledge that the reflective light, looking like a bright ball, is centered on the mirror.

From the backseat, "Fog."

We're traveling at 160 mph descending to an invisible ship hidden in the black of night and dense fog.

At ¾ mile, we are just seconds from the conclusion of the flight, whatever it may be.

I let my eyes peak up from my instrument panel, nothing but fog and dark.

I shoot back to the LSO, "Negative mirror."

Again from the backseat, "Fog."

Then some unusual, yet supportive, words from the LSO, "Keep it coming you *sound* good."

Sound good? I thought.

Input after input. 160 mph. Night. Fog. Trust. Faith. Discernment.

Finally, at ¼ mile, less than six seconds from landing and only 200 feet above the water, I hear the magic word from the backseat, "Clear!" We're finally through the fog.

Due to security, the carrier looks nothing like a Carnival Cruise ship with millions of lights. The carrier is all but dark with only a long string of red lights hanging from the backside of the ship to help the pilot to line up for landing.

If the pilot has taken the overwhelming number of inputs and imparted them into the flying of the plane, the hanging red lights, and the mirror, with a "centered ball" should be there.

A quick input from the LSO, a minor adjustment to the aircraft power and rudders, the aircraft hits the deck and the "tailhook," a metal scoop hanging from the back of the aircraft, grabs the several-inch-thick cable bringing us to an immediate stop, as if a controlled crash.

Why all of this detail? Because daily life is not much different from what I just described with one additional caveat: In the case of the night carrier landing, each input was "trusted" to be *positive.* In real life, we are bombarded with an infinite number of inputs, both *positive* and *negative.* Positive. Negative. How do we know what is right?

I believe that we, as humans versus animals, are given one additional gift. It is discernment. The freedom to choose.

Unfortunately it is getting harder each day to discern properly since so much of the daily input is now *negative.* Who discerns for our children? When I was young, we were taught not to go into the street and if we lived on a farm to respect the equipment we were around. Our parents had little need to monitor the TV shows or worry about the lyrics in a best selling song. They did not need to worry about the influx of pornography.

What about today? Discernment is more important than ever. We must look at our own lives first to see what input we are receiving and what are we doing with that input. Then we are in a position to discern for our kids.

Fog. Night. High speed. Low altitude. Sure, coming aboard ship at night is scary. An unwillingness to discern the inputs will usually cause catastrophic consequences. Not a lot different than everyday life.

Patience

I have yet to meet a person who has not experienced pain or problems in their lives.

As a therapist I would meet people on a daily basis who were dealing with loss, health issues, financial shortfalls, marital or family problems, and just about anything else.

For most of us who struggle, we seek either professional help or the ear of a friend.

The problem with problems is that they often take a considerable amount of time to solve. Remember that most problems grow a little at a time until they became overwhelming and the solution would be just the reverse.

If one deals with grief, relief comes a little at a time as one replaces the painful loss with buried memories.

If one deals with alcoholism or drug abuse, the solution comes with 12-Step meetings day after day. In time, the addicted person will replace the illusionary god, the alcohol or drug, with a power greater than the alcohol or drug.

Marital solutions demand that one learn to listen, listen, and listen. It means the dissolving of the illusion that "it is all about me" and a replacement of commitment to each other.

Financial problems don't go away easily. They dissolve a few dollars at a time with a long-term commitment.

Expanded health arrives when one evaluates what is eaten and drank, and then replacing our intake with something more nutritious.

You may have noticed that each of these requires a large block of time to reach a solution. That is the hardest part because we are a country of the "free and the brave" and the impatient.

Yes, impatience has become the cornerstone of our existence. "I want what I want and when I want it. And that is right now."

So, for most of us the potential solution to a problem starts with the tackling of the word "patience."

If one shuts down the grieving process, the sacred memories from times past may never be discovered.

If one only attends a few 12-Step meetings before concluding that the program is not for them, long term sobriety may never be achieved.

If one chooses divorce court before allowing the process of "listening" to take hold, a loving lifelong relationship may never be discovered.

If one chooses bankruptcy without attempting to work out credit arrangements with the creditors, decades of bad credit reports may follow.

In addition, if I don't commit to a healthy diet, medical consequences may arise.

Unfortunately, impatience does not blend well with the recommended long term solutions. In fact, impatience often causes us to give up too soon. Unfortunately, impatience may cause us to quit before the miracle ever happens.

Are You Using Duct Tape?

Recently I heard Minister Rob Bell say, "Your words describing what you stand for are nice, but do your actions follow your words?"

Rob went a step further by handing out strips of duct tape and metaphorically suggested the congregation cover their mouths with the tape. This question then followed: With the tape over your mouth would anyone recognize you from your earlier words?

While the great religions of the world all speak of God's love, would we recognize any of them if they were all mandated to wear duct tape?

Over time I have come to believe that religion is man made while spirituality is God given and a connection between religion and the love of God is often hard to find.

Maybe we have a misguided notion that connecting religion with the love of God might be the same as connecting a wedding day with a happy marriage. They both make good starting points but neither guarantees a loving outcome.

In the 1980's Dr. Merkle used to say something about marriage that certainly could be applied to religion as well: "Every marriage has to eventually have a divorce." His belief, and I fully agree, was that all couples, at the beginning of a relationship, come together out of need. "I bring something you need, while you bring something I need." Unfortunately, these "needs" eventually become less fulfilling than earlier in the relationship. Therefore, his divorce was not the kind you do in court, but rather a decision to divorce from the earlier "needs" and the rediscovering of each other at a higher, more spiritual, place.

If religion, like marriage, does not evolve from its starting point to a deeper relationship with God, it will be doomed for failure as well. The churchgoer will come to accept a Sunday seat in church with frequent looks at the watch, just as the wedding partners survive each day by "just putting up with each other."

Visualize the duct tape. If your priest, minister, or rabbi put it over his or her mouth, would we still recognize their actions based on their earlier words?

What about us?

Life and Experiences

Life. It is nothing but experiences, experiences, and experiences.

In my case, some of them have been good and some of them have been bad. Whether good or bad, they have all helped me to be the person I have become at this very moment.

Accepting that, I can then say that with all that I have experienced, none of it has been wasted. It has all been part of the process to move toward my spiritual purpose.

What is purpose? I am of the opinion that our only purpose in life is to become loving. Others say, "God made us for a particular purpose."

I have read numerous times that "God is love." Others believe that we are created in the image and likeness of God. If so, then our image and likeness should be nothing but love.

If our only purpose is to be loving, then why is it we struggle so much with it?

Could it be that our biggest struggle is with the expression of purpose, or love?

Years ago a movie, ***Chariots of Fire***, swept the country. It was a true story about running, Olympics, success, failure, and purpose.

Several young men were approaching the same Olympic games, each with a different motive.

"I need to win or else."

"I will do anything to win."

"I run because it's my purpose. It is my method of expressing God's love through the gift God has given me."

Maybe our problem with purpose is more in the expression of it, or the expression of love.

At different times, I have felt the same emotions of each of these young men, but as I have gotten older, I have tried to focus on the purpose expressed in the latter statement.

The runner knew his purpose, but he also understood the strength to be living his purpose came from a power greater than himself. It came from within, at the place which connects to the limitless energy of God.

That seems to be the key. Our purpose is loving and it can be expressed in a multitude of ways, but the energy to express that purpose has to come from somewhere other than from ourselves. I suspect that would be the place of limitless energy, God.

Who is God?

Who is God and what does God think and look like? I don't know about you, but I can do all the speculating I want and can find more than a few sources that will substantiate any perception I may have.

Does your God look like an old man with whiskers or maybe a female? Maybe you've concluded there is no God.

I've struggled with the concept of God all of my life. I've read, studied, and talked to more than a few people about their concept, mostly people of the cloth.

Recently a famous Jewish leader in Israel had a serious stroke. Contrary to his past policy, he was working endlessly to find a route to peace with the Palestinians.

I may be wrong, but I would guess that he probably set himself up for the stroke being terribly overweight, as well as having high blood pressure.

On the other hand, if I choose to believe a world famous "minister" of God I would be wrong. This minister decided to speak for God and tell all of us that the reason the leader of Israel had a stroke was because he was about to give "God's" land away to the Palestinians. This land, according to him, was God's land and only the Jewish people could own it.

Do you know why 9-11 occurred? According to another famous minister, the reason for 9-11 was due to God's anger at all of the gays working in the towers.

If one is struggling to find a loving God in their lives, how can they do it with leadership like that?

What about the 10,000 cases of priests sexually abusing children?

The same minister who decreed the Jewish people's mistake also suggested that someone should kill the president of Venezuela. Since this minister was Christian, and supposedly a mirror image of Jesus, I have great difficulty in imagining that Jesus would have called for a "hit" on any of the leaders in the Roman Empire.

Granted, most people of the cloth are good and genuine people, but let's not forget that God doesn't just live in a church as some would make you think. The spirit of God lives within each of us, available at any moment, with or without the help of someone else.

Religion is not the Magic Word

My early religious training taught me to be fearful and scared of God. I was told that if I wanted to get to heaven I needed to be nearly perfect. Further, there would be a review of my "final exam," graded by St. Peter at the Gates of Heaven. Only then would I be told if I was going to heaven or hell.

If I was sent to "hell" I would start to look like a devil, and if I went to "heaven" I would have to start wearing a white robe, sit in the clouds, and learn to play a harp. As I was taught this out of my catechism, I remember thinking that neither option sounded all that good.

I used to think that my religion must have had its beginning in some department of the Federal Government because it had at least as many rules and regulations. Unfortunately, most of the rules had their beginning in the minds of church leaders who were spring loaded to controlling the "flock" instead of exposing them to God's love.

A church's loving energy should draw people to it, not drive people away.

I also knew that I could never live up to what was expected to "theoretically" receive God's love.

Somewhere in the Bible it talks of imagining "loving parents." Then imagine how much more loving God would be!

My parents were always loving and if God would be an expansion of their love, then we would be on the right path. I could never imagine that my parents would have created all these rules, giving me "free will," and then telling me I would burn in hell if I did not follow their "just conceived rules."

Sure, I attended church when I was young because it was a rule, not because I was being fed with spiritual growth. I remember arguing with my uncle when I was young suggesting, "Instead of sitting in a church, wouldn't it be better if we were out helping people instead?"

I, like so many people my age, left the church when we finally could. Even though the church seldom fed me, there remained a yearning, a gnawing, coming from the inside. On occasion, I would return to the church of my roots, hoping that something would have changed and that I would have grown to believe what the church believed. With each visit, I knew I was growing further away. I would look around the church and all I could see were hundreds of people looking at their watches, wondering how much longer the service would take.

However, the gnawing never stopped and I knew there had to be more to my spiritual life than what I had experienced up until then. I looked. I searched. I asked questions. I tried different churches. Nothing. I went back to the old church. Nothing.

Expressing this frustration to a friend, she recommended a church with a lot of energy. Energy? Interesting statement.

I went.

Within minutes I knew this was the place that my heart had been crying for. The minister, Pastor Mike, had a son that was a baseball player. I had two.

He stated that it was "about relationship, not religion." He talked of helping others, not just sitting on our butts in church. He talked of God's unlimited grace, like a well of loving water that would never run dry. He talked of a relationship with God, like that with our parents, but so much more.

I no longer had to worry about this "final exam" and then a one-way ticket "up" or "down."

I knew I was finally home and it was a home that had always been there for me. A home with a loving and unconditional God, not a God of revenge.

Unusual Hitchhiker

I often talk of my many trips up and down the mountain from my home in Lytle Creek.

Often my trip includes a hitchhiker or two. I've written about the night I stopped and instead of the rider opening the front door, he opened the back door, scaring me to death as he and his dogs jumped in.

I've written about the young man who would play his guitar up and down the hill. I haven't seen him in a long time. I wonder what happened to him.

Each time I stopped to offer a ride I had to make a conscious decision to be helpful and would have to act in trust and faith that the person I picked up did not have an ulterior motive.

Most times the gut-feel decision was simple and with little thought.

The other night I went to a much-awaited seminar to listen to a nationally-known speaker.

I went with anticipation because everyone talked about how moved they were after having heard her. Although the seminar ended up being exceptional, the first night was not at the level I had hoped. With disappointment and an early morning commitment the following day, I wanted the seminar to end and I wanted to go home.

By the time I started up my hill, I was not much of a spiritual person. Therefore, when I came across a hitchhiker I decided to ignore him. Besides, the hitchhiker looked like he may have been drinking as he was weaving on the edge of the road.

Without warning, my head started a conversation

with my heart. "No, this person is on their own tonight."

If I'm frustrated, I'm going to take it out on someone and tonight this hitchhiker is the recipient.

I went around the next bend and a small voice leaked out of my being, "why?"

Why what?

"Why didn't you pick this person up?"

I didn't feel like it.

"Why?"

I just don't feel like it.

"That could easily be you."

So?

I didn't like the seminar.

"So?"

I'm already a mile past the hitchhiker.

"So?"

Someone else will stop.

"Are you sure?"

I don't care.

"You don't?"

Damn it, I don't care.

The discussion ended as I continued up the hill.

A mile later I slowed and stopped, allowing what had occurred to sink in.

After a few moments, I concluded this was stupid and I needed to get out of my head and back to my heart.

I maneuvered, turned the car around, and headed back down the hill.

When my headlights again picked up the hitchhiker, still struggling to walk a straight line, I again turned around and pulled up next to the walker. The door opened and I was shocked to find that "he" was a "she."

All she could say was "Thank you for stopping. It is so cold. Thank you for stopping. It is so cold."

"Are you okay?"

"I am so cold."

As she stood next to the car door I could see she had her arms full with a backpack and a box with a coat over the top of it.

Before she crawled in the front seat, she put her backpack in the back seat. She was holding a box covered by her coat.

"I'm so cold."

"If you are cold, why aren't you wearing your coat?"

"I've got a cockatoo in the box and she's cold, too. Oh, thank God you stopped."

We started up the hill as she continued to bounce between thanking me, talking to the bird, telling me how cold she was, and an occasional comment to an imaginary friend that was traveling with her in her mind.

She told me she had been walking for hours and no one would pick her up. She concluded with one more, "Thank you."

With each mile the resentment of the seminar dissipated. With each mile, I knew that my powerful ego nearly prevented me from helping this person on a secluded mountain road, late at night, with a temperature hovering around 30 degrees. My ego could have seriously hurt this person.

Would someone have picked her up? I don't know.

I stopped to drop her off at a trailer park about a mile from my home. As she first lifted her 30-pound backpack out of the back seat and then the birdcage, she offered one more "thank you" as the door closed and she was gone.

As she walked in front of the car, I remembered the staggering I had seen earlier. She continued to limp, but not because of drugs or alcohol. She clearly had been afflicted with something like cerebral palsy.

What a night. I try so hard to not let ego run my life and most times I fail. Tonight I almost did.

Rules or Free Will

One of the greatest gifts all of us have been given is free will. However, “free will” is accompanied by “rules. “

I'm not talking about the rules that tell us that the arbitrary speed limit on this road is “55 mph” or “45 mph.” I am speaking of universal rules that are interwoven into the DNA of the spiritual universe.

I have spent all of my life fumbling, tripping, and falling as I have tried to learn some of the “universal rules.” Then when I do finally learn one of the rules, I wonder why I didn’t choose to accept the rule sooner.

A big shift in my spiritual learning came when I accepted that “giving and receiving are one and the same.” To someone else, this rule may still be only words.

Another one that brought me peace was the realization that “only love is real, everything else is fake.”

Let me say again, there are many universal rules and they all apply to each of us, but they only become of value when we come to integrate them into our lives. Unfortunately, if you are like me, you will integrate them only after everything else has failed.

I have done a couple projects with the Benedictine Monks in California. They were founded by St. Benedict who guided his followers with a set of rules that eventually became known as the Rules of St. Benedict.

One of the rules states, “Listen carefully, my son, to the Master’s instructions, and attend to them with the ear of your heart.”

In my journaling, I suspect that much of what I

write about is my acceptance or struggle with the universal rules.

In the 12-Step programs they talk of living "one day at a time." Others cut it down even further by suggesting that one "needs to live in the moment." Integration of this may be the most important thing to do to maintain one's sobriety.

I read a book entitled ***God Calling***, edited by A.J. Russell. Much of what is in the book is what I aspire to, but seems so far away. For example, today's reading includes the words, "Pray Daily for Faith. It is My gift." For many this is already integrated into their daily life.

I continue to struggle with it.

The Mystery of Finding Self

Do you enjoy the "solve them" types of mysteries on TV? I love them.

I grew up with the ***Perry Mason*** mysteries on Saturday nights shown only in black and white. I was always disappointed because I could never figure out "who done it" before Perry would undercover the right person with just the right questions, and magically just after the last commercial.

I have seen every ***Columbo*** mystery, and I'm certain I have seen nearly every ***Matlock*** show as well. Most of them several times.

I suspect that our spiritual transformation is a lot like a detective solving a mystery.

I'm of the opinion that a mystery is nothing more than the discovery of the "final suspect," while spiritual transformation is the discovery of who we really are.

How did Perry always get his man or woman? Through his private investigator, Paul Drake, he would investigate all of the people who might have a motive. Over time, through vigorous investigation, each of the possible suspects would be removed from the "possible list" because of their alibi. In other words, he would reach his conclusion by removing people until there was only one person left. Over time, he would find the true culprit.

Coming to know oneself is done in very much the same way. At the beginning, we are an accumulation of many different levels of ego, each sending the world a different picture. If Perry were to question us, he would probably have great difficulty in understanding who we really are. However, if he were a therapist instead of an attorney, he might be able to cut through the many levels, and over time and with hard work he would help us to see the real person buried somewhere within us.

Perry the therapist may not be available, but there are many avenues to start looking at one's self. Most of them start by just becoming honest with ourselves. If we are willing to do this, we will eventually find the "real self" just as Perry would find the "real culprit."

When we do find that person, what will we find? Simple. Look in the mirror and the person we see will look very much like the original person, probably identical. However, if we look a bit closer, we will see something more. It will be our "true self," made in the image and likeness of God.

Epilogue

Recently I celebrated 26 years in a 12-Step program that continues to provide me with an unending and unconditional method of support.

When celebrating any type of 12-Step birthday, whether it be for 30 days, 60 days, one year, or 26, there is a traditional question that is asked by the group: "How did you do it?"

When asked the question, I responded with an answer that took some of the listeners off guard: "I didn't."

After pausing for a few seconds, I then went on to say, "That is correct. I didn't do it. I only provided a willingness to step aside and let a Power greater than I do it.

"The sum of all my abilities could not control my drinking. The sum of all my abilities could not keep me out of trouble. Likewise, the sum of all my abilities could never 'fix' all that I had caused.

"I am here today because of my willingness to let go of all my 'inabilities' and replace them with a Power that was able."

26 years of meetings. Am I just a slow learner? Maybe. For me, dismantling the ego will take a lifetime. Some of my friends say it will take more than one life in my case.

Where do I go from here? For me to have daily peace of mind:

-I must continue to have faith and trust in a Power greater than myself, namely an all-loving God.

-I must continue to work on myself chipping away at anything that is not of God, in other words, anything that is not loving.

-I must continue to help others.

Although this is the final reflection in this book, it is by no means a conclusion. It is merely a reflective snapshot along the journey, a lifelong journey that has taken me back to God, a God who has never left me.

Serenity has been creating music and guided imagery for relaxation, and now DVDs, since 1985.

A world leader in relaxation music, **Serenity's** customers include massage therapists, day spas, yoga instructors, doctors, nurses, dentists, stress and pain clinics, childbirth educators, counselors, school teachers, music therapists, health food stores, Hospice professionals, and many others.

Our music has also traveled to some unique places. **Good Morning America** has often used our music while **General Motors** has used us in commercials. Many years ago, then **President Ronald Reagan** took our music along to the Soviet Union as a gift for **President Gorbechev.**

Most have heard of **Yanni**. **Serenity** artist **Shardad Rohani** arranged and orchestrated his music, and conducted the symphony orchestra for **Yanni-Live at the Acropolis.**

For further information:

www.SerenityMusic.com or

Call (800)869-1684